Law and Disorder

Leo M. Franklin
1870-1948

Law and Disorder

The Legitimation of Direct Action as an
Instrument of Social Policy

The Franklin Memorial Lectures
Volume XIX

Compiled by Samuel I. Shuman
Holder of the Leo M. Franklin Memorial
Lectureship in Human Relations
at Wayne State University for the year 1968–1969

Detroit—Wayne State University Press—1971

Grateful acknowledgment is made to Temple Beth El for
financial assistance in publishing this volume to commemorate
Rabbi Leo M. Franklin, the spiritual leader of Temple Beth
El from 1899 to 1941 and Rabbi Emeritus thereafter till his
death in 1948.

The Leo M. Franklin Lectures and the Holders of the Leo M. Franklin Memorial Lectureship in Human Relations at Wayne State University

†Vol. I	(1951)	**Toward Better Human Relations** Lloyd Allen Cook, *Professor of Educational Sociology*
Vol. II *	(1952)	**Our Troubles with Defiant Youth** Fritz Redl, *Professor of Social Work*
†Vol. III	(1953)	**American Foreign Policy and American Democracy** Alfred H. Kelly, *Professor of History*
†Vol. IV	(1954)	**Contemporary Problems in Religion** Harold A. Basilius, *Professor of German*
†Vol. V	(1955)	**Problems of Power in American Democracy** Arthur Kornhauser, *Professor of Psychology*
†Vol. VI	(1956)	**The City in Mid-Century** H. Warren Dunham, *Professor of Sociology*
Vol. VII	(1957)	**The Nature of Being Human** Marie I. Rasey, *Professor of Educational Psychology*

7

Vol. VIII   (1958)   **Twentieth-Century Pessimism and the American Dream**
Raymond C. Miller, *Professor of History*

Vol. IX   (1959)   **Preserving Human Values in an Age of Technology**
Edgar G. Johnston, *Professor of Education*

Vol. X   (1960)   **The Growth of Self-Insight**
John M. Dorsey, *University Professor*

Vol. XI   (1961)   **The Horizons of Man**
Marion Edman, *Professor of Education*

Vol. XII   (1962)   **New Horizons of Economic Progress**
Lawrence H. Seltzer, *Professor of Economics*

Vol. XIII   (1963)   **Mid-Twentieth Century Nationalism**
William J. Bossenbrook, *Professor of History*

Vol. XIV   (1964)   **All Men are Created Equal**
William W. Wattenberg, *Professor of Educational Psychology*

Vol. XV   (1965)   **The Dimensions of Human Conflict**
Ross Stagner, *Professor of Psychology*

Vol. XVI*   (1966)   **Self-Identity in an Uncertain World**
Mildred Peters, *Professor of Guidance and Counseling*

Vol. XVII   (1967)   **The Future of Communism in Europe**
R. V. Burks, *Professor of History*

Vol. XVIII* (1968)   **The Rights of Children and Youth**
David Wineman, *Professor of Sociology*

† *Out of print.*   * *Unpublished.*
Titles of volumes differ in some instances from titles of lectures as originally announced.

Preface

Dr. Leo M. Franklin served as rabbi to Temple Beth El from *1899* until *1941* and as Rabbi Emeritus until his death in *1948*. He was widely recognized for his leadership within the Detroit community and had a national reputation for his work in the field of human relations. To perpetuate his memory and his interest and contributions in the field of human relations, in *1950* Temple Beth El made a grant to Wayne State University. That grant and subsequent ones from the Temple have made possible the annual Leo M. Franklin Memorial Lecture Series. Since their creation in *1950*, this series has been recognized as the most important annual series of lectures offered within the university.

Each year a faculty committee recommends to the president of the university one faculty member whom the president then names as the Franklin Memorial Professor. In that capacity the Professor arranges for the lecture series and contributes at least one of the lectures himself. The lectures which follow were delivered at Wayne State University during the spring of *1969*. I hope that their subject is responsive to the seriousness of the problem to which they are addressed.

The lectures are presented essentially as delivered except that three of the lectures are expanded here.

I am much honored to have been chosen Franklin Memo-

rial Professor for *1969*. To the faculty who made the recom-
mendation and to President Keast who confirmed it, I express
my thanks for having thus honored me.

S. I. Shuman

Contents

11

Introduction

In searching for a subject which would be consistent with the general theme of the Franklin Lectures, that is, human relations, I thought none more appropriate than the increasing concern with what has come to be called "law and order." The demand for more order, which is generally equated with the notion that more law will produce more order, has been heard with increasing frequency, at least since the presidential election of 1968. The range of conduct encompassed within the notions of order and disorder and the strength of the conviction as to what can be accomplished by law have varied in recent years. In addition, it is difficult to isolate the phenomena with a sufficient degree of precision even to identify what are really the central demands for law and order. Against a background of growing tension because of the apparent lack of order and with a concern for developing some strategy to accomplish those legitimate social objectives which seem to be paramount in the minds of many, the topic of "Law and Disorder" is almost a natural section for these lectures.

As a focus for the lectures each speaker concerns himself with the problem of action as a vehicle for expressing ideas and with the questions generated by conduct which is purportedly expressive. While much of the cry for law and order is directed towards the usual forms of antisocial conduct, much of the present outcry is directed not towards these but towards violent expressive conduct which is used with increasing frequency as a means for expressing political sentiments. I thought it appropriate, therefore, to focus on this phase of the demand for law and order and to see how far law has, could, or should reflect the demand for order, even when such order may require suppression of the right to freedom of expression by speech or conduct. Protests for political, social or moral objectives are hardly new, but the increasingly imaginative exploitation of protest conduct and the wider use of protest conduct in order to dramatize an issue and compel a confrontation have generated a new colony of problems. It is to some of these problems that these lectures are directed.

While expressive conduct need not be identified with violence—indeed it is probably an exaggeration even to say that a large percentage of such conduct does accompany or generate violence—it is that segment of expressive conduct which has and is likely to generate violence which is generally of primary concern. Whether or not statistically justified, in the minds of many persons there seems to be a connection between violence and demonstrative expressive conduct.

In the first lecture, Justice Clark canvasses some of the history of violence in the United States and does so against the background of legal decisions. In the second lecture, I offer an analysis of recent Supreme Court decisions wherein the Court has responded to cases generated by the wave of recent direct actions in which the participants purport to express views about political or social objective. Particularly since the sit-in cases of the early 60's has the Supreme Court been required to respond to the increasing number of cases produced by direct action. It is primarily these cases that I attempt to analyze to discover the developments in protest by direct action.

In the third lecture, Dr. van den Haag offers a number of social and psychological insights into the general phenomena with which we are concerned, in some places focusing on student activism and in other places examining a wider political field. His generally critical attack on what he regards as excessive demonstrative conduct is almost a classical statement of the position he wishes to defend. Professor Charles Hamilton presents an almost classical response to that position. In the fourth lecture, Hamilton is particularly concerned to show the appropriateness of demonstrative expressive conduct in the cause of black freedom and equality. In the last lecture I attempt to deal with the relevance of direct action within the context of the attack on the traditional role of the universities.

It would be presumptuous to maintain that any series of five lectures could adequately respond to the enormous problems with which we are here concerned. However, it is my hope that the lectures provide some illumination of the character of the problems we confront, as well as some insight into the alternatives available for the resolution of the tensions generated by these problems.

I

Some Historical Antecedents
for the Use of Direct Action

by
Tom C. Clark
Associate Justice
U. S. Supreme Court

It is a high honor and a distinct privilege for me to participate in the Leo M. Franklin Memorial Lectures in Human Relations. Now in its nineteenth year, the series has become widely and favorably known as a catalyst in promoting an "increased knowledge and better understanding of the thorny problems of intergroup relations in American urban life." The subject chosen for 1969, "Law and Disorder: The Legitimation of Direct Action as an Instrument of Social Policy" is a most timely choice, coming, as it does, in the midst of increasingly concentrated attacks upon existing social and political philosophy. "The Establishment" has suffered some reverses that are fundamental and which give renewed vigor and broader horizons to those engaged in the direct action movement. I daresay that Rabbi Franklin would hardly recognize the direct action techniques of minorities that have been developed and legitimated since his passing.

The four lecturers in the series have been assigned specific topics coming within the overall subject matter. Mine has to do with the role of the courts in the legitimation of direct action. It is my purpose to trace the development of direct action; the manner and extent to which it has attained the approval of the judicial process and its probable course in the future.

The power of an impassioned minority to disrupt the orderly processes of society has always been great but until of late has been used sparingly. This is because direct action has not long enjoyed legitimate status. While the Boston Tea Party had a profound effect upon the morale of the colonists, it was looked upon as illegitimate. There was a temporary disruption in the harbor, but it was soon dissipated by constituted authority. A repeat performance, known as the "Whiskey Rebellion" by some Pennsylvania whiskey-making farmers, had even less success. Their effort to escape a federal tax by direct action failed, but only after President Washington had dispatched 15,000 federal troops to the scene of the trouble. Forty years later, some Rhode Island rebels brought on Dorr's Rebellion as an expression of their dissatisfaction and long suffering over the failure of that state to re-apportion its legislative body. President Tyler intervened, Dorr was convicted of treason and was ordered expelled to England. He escaped but the action was dissipated. The Vigilantes, a self-constituted judicial body, was first organized in the gold fields of California in 1851. The rapid increase of crime and a breakdown of law enforcement brought about the organization of a committee of some 200 members which later increased in size. Within 30 days four desperadoes were taken into custody by the Vigilance Committee, tried and hanged. Others were banished from the community. The movement spread into Idaho and Montana.

Riots, assaults and persecutions were visited upon the Abolitionists in their efforts to free the slaves. The movement was disrupted, but William Lloyd Garrison, Wendell Phillips, Lucretia Mott and John Brown—its leaders—continued their direct action until the most destructive civil war in history broke out over John Brown's body. It was during that struggle that a direct action group gained some concession from Congress, i.e., that a draftee might substitute a professional soldier for himself and thus escape service. This method of buying one's way out of army service was, perhaps, the first successful direct action program in our history. It was achieved only after a bloody riot—affecting hundreds of people—ran its course in

New York City. History says that Abraham Lincoln effected the compromise. After the swords of the Civil War "were beaten into plow shares," other direct action groups acting clandestinely grew up in the South. Taking the law into their own hands and with hood and cloak to hide themselves from detection, they rode highways and byways leaving death, injury and terror in their wake. They were known as the Ku Klux Klan, the Knights of the White Camellia, the Pale Faces and the Invisible Empire of the South. Thomas Hobbes once said that those "who live outside of organized society are poor, mean, nasty, brutish and short-lived." The activities of these self-appointed marauders aptly filled that description.

The Fourteenth Amendment was adopted in 1868. However, the courts did not accord it even lip service for over a half century. A series of Supreme Court opinions practically repealed the Amendment. The *Civil Rights Cases* limited its enforcement to state action; *Plessy v. Ferguson* created the separate but equal doctrine in education; the *Slaughter House* case rendered the privileges and immunity clause a nullity; *Munn v. Illinois* stripped the due process clause of its power over the excesses of the states; *Giles v. Harris* disenfranchised the Negroes and *Colegrove v. Green* doomed re-apportionment without invidious discrimination. Thus our educational, economic, social and political life was strait-jacketed by the age old philosophy of discrimination.

This conditioning brought on more direct action. Around the turn of the century Cox's Army marched on Washington without success. Labor problems became acute and the Sherman Anti-trust Law was turned on Eugene Debs, a militant labor leader. Ironically, a law aimed at curbing corporate power became the instrument of control of a growing labor movement. The Bonus Marchers tormented President Hoover into calling out troops to literally run the marchers out of Washington. You will remember the news media carrying pictures of General Douglas MacArthur, Chief of Staff of the

Army and his Aide, Dwight Eisenhower, overseeing the forced evacuation which was effected by the use of tanks. This show of strength, however, did not seem to dampen the spirit of the country's automobile workers. A few years later, they took over physically one of General Motors' main plants in Flint and held it hostage for days, despite the violence of strike breakers. It was only through the final intervention of Governor Frank Murphy that the melee was settled. It was the first great victory for the forces of direct action. Meanwhile, John Lewis, another intrepid leader of the new labor movement, was not so successful in the coal fields of Harlan County, Kentucky. A veritable armed insurrection took place there between opposing labor forces. The Norris-LaGuardia Act exempting labor from the Sherman Law had tipped the scales the other way. Big labor began flexing its muscles more successfully.

In the meanwhile *Gitlow v. New York* had visited the First Amendment's free speech and press provisions against the states on the basis that free speech and press were among the fundamental personal rights protected by the due process clause of the 14th Amendment. Earlier (1897) the Court had applied the just compensation requirement of the Fifth Amendment as to the public taking of private property against the states but it had steadfastly refused to do so as to personal rights. *Gitlow* was the breaking point of the laissez-faire philosophy that the Court had been following for many years. *Cantwell v. Connecticut* soon followed, and an enlightened era was on its way.

Negro civil rights leaders saw the handwriting on the wall and began a judicial attack on segregation practices. This bore fruit in *Sweatt v. Painter* in graduate education and *Brown v. Board of Education* in the elementary schools. There followed a painful period of interposition and massive resistance to *Brown's* requirements. I remember well that the governor of Virginia announced soon after the *Brown* opinion that his state would, of course, obey the rulings of the Supreme Court. However, this position eroded and soon the Old Dominion—so much beloved and respected in the South—gave in to the resistance. This had a direct impact upon other Southern states and, I believe, was the cause of much of the resulting delay and physical confrontation. You will remember the defiant attitude of Governors Wallace, Faubus and Barnett in trying to prevent the integration of the universities of their respective states. Their public confrontation with the law not only reverberated around the world but had much to do with sparking our present day riot problem. If the governors of three states could use their high offices in disobedience to the law and the specific order of a court, why could not an individual or a group? Theirs was a sorry spectacle requiring the calling out of federal troops to quell a riot led by the constituted authority of the state!

Soon direct action began in other areas, such as transportation, recreation and public accommodation. Soon this, too, splashed over into violence and a rash of cases came to the Court. Segregation statutes of the states were stricken again and again. Indeed, I remember only two argued cases in which convictions were affirmed. Finally, *Hamm* and *Lupper* ordered several hundred convictions set aside and the cases dismissed in the light of the public accommodation act of the Congress.

Many people misunderstood these holdings, believing that the Court was reaching out in an effort to stop state action. This is not true. Unlike a legislative body, the Court cannot pass a rule whenever a majority of its members wish. It must wait until a suit or controversy reaches it. This is what we call a lawsuit—a justiciable issue. Moreover, the lawsuit must involve a substantial federal question arising under the Constitution, the laws or a treaty of the United States. Furthermore, if the lawsuit comes from a state court, the Court must wait until the court of last resort of the state has decided it. If the lawsuit originates in the federal courts, the Court cannot pass on it, as a general rule, until it is decided by both the District Court and the Court of Appeals. This usually involves a wait of some two years. Finally, the Court actually decides only a few cases on the merits—slightly over 200 a term. However, over 3000 cases are filed each term. The remainder are handled under a certiorari system that was approved by the Congress back in 1927. Under it each justice studies each case personally but unless as many as four of them vote to hear an argument in it, the matter is disposed of summarily. The result is that the Court actually writes on less than 7 percent of the cases brought there. The delay in final adjudication, I am sure, causes many litigants not to take their lawsuits to the Supreme Court.

The American people are dilatory in more ways than in litigation. They invariably delay making difficult decisions. Take the Constitutional Convention of 1787. When it came to the abolition of slavery, they took the easy course. Article I Section 2 in its final form was a pure compromise. It provided that in the taking of a census, only three fifths of those human beings in slavery were to be counted. All of the delegates to the Convention, I am sure, knew that slavery should be abolished. It violated the very principle upon which they were founding the United States. Still those who fought for the abolition of slavery finally decided that they would have to delay the abolition of it if there was to be a United States of America. Wanting dearly to create a new nation, they finally compromised. Later the Congress did likewise in the Missouri Compromise. Even Abraham Lincoln proposed that the Union buy up the slaves and turn them free. This propensity of ours not to face up to trouble is often our undoing. In this case it brought on the Civil War.

Likewise in our court system we are compromising with justice. The injustices of justice are many. In fact, we have many laws but little justice. Let me give you an example. In Washington, D. C., only last year a salesman was making the rounds of a poor neighborhood—not a ghetto but still not a desirable section. He would knock on the door and gain admittance on the ruse that he was giving away a Bible. After entering and reading a verse or so from the Bible, he would offer it as a gift. Finally, when the housewife accepted, the salesman would advise her that he needed a receipt. However, this paper was an order form for periodicals. She signed it without reading the content. A month or so after the periodicals began to come, the housewife got a summons to the General Sessions Court. She went down on the appointed day and found the courtroom crowded. Her case was called about noon. She went to the bench and was explaining the matter to the judge when a lawyer came up, told the judge he thought that he could work it out. The judge suggested the lawyer and the housewife go into the corner of the courtroom and talk it over. They did this and soon another lady came up who the housewife thought was attached to the court. She told the housewife that she must pay and finally the latter agreed to pay one dollar a week out of her welfare allowance. The lawyer returned to the bench alone and a judgment was entered. A month later an officer called on the housewife to collect the judgment and failing to do so, levied on her household goods. The housewife then took the matter to legal aid and through some young students there was able to get the judgment set aside. How many thousands of times does this occur over the nation? But without such a happy ending!

Our courts of general jurisdiction are plagued with the same problem of congestion. Their trials are so badly delayed that justice is often denied. It is a common practice to find a case on the docket over three years before reaching trial and sometimes the time lag runs over five years. This prevents any one short on funds from using the judicial process. He cannot stand such inordinate delay in the pursuit of justice. And for one who is deprived of constitutional rights, it is a denial of those rights. Oliver Brown was in the courts for a decade before *Brown v. Board of Education* finally came down. I doubt if his child ever attended an integrated school. Millions of our citizens have suffered the same plight.

Procrastination has always been the rule of conduct in the

field of human needs and social justice. I believe with Justice Brandeis that most all Americans sincerely want to support themselves once they are given an opportunity to do so. Our trouble is that we do not keep the paths to jobs open. We close them through custom, law and practice. Many of the great unions—such as bricklaying—are closed; harbor pilots are in the same category; buildings trades are mostly white; and machines have driven the common laborer from the market. We must upgrade these citizens into skilled trades, open up the membership of every union and eliminate all discrimination in hiring practices. Every American has a clear and unmistakable duty to require fair and decent treatment of his fellowman. Every physically able adult who wishes to work must be found a job or trained to fill one; every juvenile must be required to attend school, and if his abilities are not commensurate with his task, he must be vocationally trained; every man, woman and child must have equal opportunity to earn his own place in a just and fair society.

This eternal delay and continued procrastination has led many of our unfortunate fellow citizens to conclude that the use of normal processes is useless and unavailing. During the past 12 months, the grim litany of events has brought on a slough of despondency among these victimized people that in the words of Hamlet has "drained the cup of [their] misery to despair." The black apostle of the underprivileged—Dr. Martin Luther King—had his life snuffed out with an assassin's bullet and Robert Kennedy—his counterpart, though white—suffered the same fate. Stripped of their leaders, they turned to other means to fulfill their hopes—means of destruction, violence, pillage and rapine. Ghetto explosions in many of our cities; smoke and fire, thieving and rioting within a stone's throw of the White House; pillaging at the Capitol and the Supreme Court, and, later, a mule train dramatizing their plight within the shadow of the Washington Monument upon the grounds of which had been erected "Resurrection City," soon condemned to destruction.

Then, too, there was the Vietnam conflict that divided our people on a hotly debated, ill-defined issue, the situs of which was thousands of miles away. The draft raised its ugly head, causing some 9000 of our young men to take refuge on foreign soil. Others took refuge in a hippy seclusion that was both incomprehensible and offensive. Still others remaining behind were assaulting the bastions of their own education, destroying themselves behind a camouflage of phony demands.

Finally came the revolt of the adults against the excesses of their young, blaming the latter on everything imaginable, except—of course—themselves! The white backlash has now turned black, and the man who fanned up both is still exacting concessions from those not versed in demagoguery.

And so it went. Nor are the crises past. Every newspaper brings front page headlines of our fragmented society—the schisms of the races and of the generations, and the cries of the poor and underprivileged. And the T. V. aggravates the situation with "Marlboro Country" tobacco advertising relating our plush society to a cancer-producing poison. A grim reminder to the indigent of their suffering at the hands of the same group.

What have we done to correct these injustices? What have we done to eliminate the violent direct action that has sprung up on all sides of us? Nothing to brag about! Indeed, we have not even cleaned up the debris left by the rioters. There has been a hue and cry for law and order. And the wailing echo to it is a plea for justice. But these calls miss the point. The issue is not law and order against justice. It is true that we cannot have order unless we have justice; and we cannot have justice unless we have order. But the choice that we must make lies between order *and* justice or chaos. I choose order and justice. Let us devote ourselves to the correction of the injustices of our justice and we shall have order. To eliminate racial and social differences in employment, housing, education and every day living must be our target. To reach this target will take much more than dollars. It will require a complete reversal of attitudes. We must turn our hearts from enmity to friendship, from distrust to trust, from disappointment to expectation, from hindrance to aid, from stark promises to full reality.

History teaches us that those unjustly held under the heel of authority continually rebel until the injustices are relieved. As Alfred North Whitehead tells us, "from the moment of birth we are immersed in action and can only fitfully guide it by taking thought." And W. G. Sumner wisely declares: "Men begin with acts, not with thoughts." Those who use violent action in an effort to secure claimed rights must think before they act. Rather than wrecking our society they must reform and correct it. Violence is not the answer; it will but destroy the very thing they seek—justice. Rather than securing redress they will only get repression. Our Constitution does not recognize an absolute and uncontrollable liberty. Individual rights can be pushed to where the action becomes self-destructive. Those who take the law into their own hands and seek by violence to expedite needed change not only jeopardize their quest but place their own lives in peril. "Lawlessness begets lawlessness," my brother Frankfurter reminds us, and "if not checked is the precursor of anarchy." It was this dilemma that Abraham Lincoln so fervently spoke of at the Lyceum Club in 1828, when he declared no man nor group is above the law nor below its protection. Though one's cause be a holy grail, there is no justification for seeking it through unlawful means. We have orderly processes—though they be slow and exasperating—through which to redress our grievances.

On the other hand, constituted authority must remember that there is more to civil liberty than a claim to the protection of the law. There must be an equality and fairness in its execution. The injustices of justice must be eliminated; the agonies of the inner cities must be corrected. To those who are condemned by the administration of the law and the heavy hand of public opinion to a hereditary state of misery and degradation we must bring not just idle talk, not empty promises, but actual and permanent relief. If this is not done, we can expect all of the passions of their frustration to rise up and riotously run through channels of self-advantage. The Bible teaches us that "for everything there is a season and a time for every purpose under Heaven." The season has come; the time is compelling. Communities are responsible as well as individuals; no government is respectable that is not just and fair. It must provide the moral tone that will set the pattern for all of its citizens. Superior strength—the use of force—cannot make wrongs into rights. As Justice Cardozo warned: "In breaking one set of shackles let us not substitute another." All power needs some restraint; practical adjustments rather than rigid formula are necessary. Only by zealously guarding the most humble, the most unorthodox and the most despised among us can freedom flourish and endure in our land.

II

Social Policy and Direct Action as Freedom of Expression

by
SAMUEL I. SHUMAN
*Professor of Law, Wayne State University
and Professor in the Department of Psychiatry,
in the School of Medicine*

1 Order and Disorder

The object of this lecture is to examine those relationships between law and disorder which affect decisions as to the kinds of direct action which may be legitimated.

Some forms of direct action have a priori legitimacy and no political process is needed to establish their status. For example, if there could be such a phenomenon as direct action requiring no overt conduct, it is likely to be legitimate, regardless of any prior or subsequent political process. (By "political" I mean legislative, judicial or executive.) Direct action, however, usually does entail overt conduct, be it as "low" level as speech or as "high" level as a deliberate and continuing trespass.

In most societies (excluding rigidly totalitarian ones), a disenchanted citizen might shake his head horizontally when told of some new repressive governmental encroachment. It is unlikely that any process will be required to legitimate that specific expression, which reluctantly could be called a direct action. But if, instead of shaking his head, he shakes a club, a judicial process may be needed to determine whether shaking clubs in certain circumstances warrants a repressive governmental action because of disorder created or threatened. What I hope to examine in the course of this lecture are those tensions between law and disorder, those forces for stability and those for change, as they affect decisions on the legitimacy of direct action. To keep the subject manageable and because most of the interesting cases are in the area of speech and expressive conduct, I shall concentrate upon that aspect of direct action phenomena.

Perhaps the issue can be sharpened if the relevant tension is more precisely identified, and rather than law and order, we speak of the polar opposites, order and disorder, and thus, in effect, equate law with order.[1] One could then ask, regarding order vs. disorder, when will direct action be legitimate? Or put differently, how much disorder will the order tolerate either because of the importance of certain types of direct action, or because of the social purpose at which the direct action is aimed, regardless of the type? There is yet a third question: Are there some social interests so exalted in the hierarchy of human values that any direct action which serves those interests comes insulated by the a priori shield of legitimacy, or at least under the presumption of such? For example, those convinced that the market place theory of ideas is of crucial significance would hold that speech is absolutely privileged, and thus speech would come insulated by the mantle of legitimacy. (I shall try to explain this in greater detail later.)

Before I analyze some illustrative cases, it will be helpful to further examine the distinction between order and disorder. Within the positivist tradition in legal or social theory, the identification of law with order is not an extreme exaggeration, since the model which is developed identifies law with order. That is, the cardinal purpose of law is to provide order, and hence if there were no order, there could be no law. To appreciate the significance of this position, it is useful to contrast the alternative theory, which may roughly be called the natural law theory. This alternative to positivism, does not do much violence to the historical developments in the general theories of legal or political philosophy. Under the natural law theory, the identification of law with order is a gross distortion, for according to that theory, the purpose of law is not to provide order but to insure justice. In such a view, the existence of order may be a necessary condition for the existence of a society in which law obtains, but it is not a sufficient condition. I do not wish to be understood as saying that for the positivist, order is both necessary and sufficient. That mistake is almost a tradition among the writers who have contrasted these two general theories, and elsewhere I have vigorously argued that this is a mistake one should avoid.[2] What I wish to stress is that between these two theories there is a significant difference in the *position* which order occupies, since for a positivist an unjust order could still be one where there is law, whereas for a natural law theorist a lawful unjust order is a contradiction in terms.

Two examples will help clarify this distinction. First, imagine a social system in which any violation, deliberate or accidental, is met by a death sentence. There are prescriptions against all of the usual crimes, rules prohibiting public speech and assembly and even rules designed to prevent social and economic mobility. Further, all power is vested in the rule makers who enforce these rules, and these rules have all of the usual indices of what we generally call law. That is, the laws were duly passed by the legislature in accordance with the fundamental constitution; they are reasonably clear, seldom retroactive, are properly promulgated, etc.[3] In a case such as this, which appears to approach the paradigm of a totalitarian, or an authoritarian, power structure, there is going to be a great deal of order, perhaps too much order. In the minds of many, South Africa, among contemporary states, typifies this kind of coercive structure. Compare with this the polar opposite, where the rules not only permit, but encourage social and economic mobility, freedom of expression and assembly, and political participation. All forms of socially deviant conduct are punished by monetary fines or other deprivations, but never by death or even long-term incarceration. While not necessarily the case, it is highly probable that in this structure there will be less order than in the first. Whether there is more justice is a matter on which the minds of reasonable men will differ. Yet, while we may differ on whether the second social system is more just *despite* the lack of order, the positivist would maintain that in the first system, there is law even though it may be repressive and produce injustice. A more interesting matter for those who regard civil disobedience as having some protected position within the legal framework is the question of whether law deserves support even when it serves the ends of injustice. It is therefore important to distinguish that which is law from that which deserves to be respected and to be very clear in saying that some rule is law but does not deserve respect. To say, on the contrary, that a certain rule does not require respect because it is not a law, is to say something very different. Fogging up this distinction obscures the difference between disobedience and legalism.[4]

The point is that there is no necessary connection between justice and order, nor is justice necessarily generated when there is order. Similarly, disorder is not necessarily incompatible with justice nor is injustice necessarily a product of either disorder or order, although there are those who would maintain that without some order, there can be no justice. That point need not be argued here for the question to which I wish to address myself is this: Within the context of the political system which obtains in the United States, when will diminution of order be warranted either because the disorder is necessary or at least useful in trying to achieve some higher justice or in trying to mitigate existing injustice? This is but a different way of asking the prior question: What are the criteria appealed to within a generally effective legal social structure when there is a question of the legitimacy of direct action? The criteria appealed to are not very obscure when it is maintained that there are some injustices not worth the disorder necessary to alleviate them because their triviality does not warrant the disruption of the existing social fabric. The more demanding question, and in a way the question at the opposite pole and for which the criteria are quite obscure is this: When, if ever, is any price in terms of disorder warranted by certain types of injustice?

The "if ever" question is answered in the affirmative by those who are willing to be civilly disobedient; but unfortunately from that commitment comes no light on the more difficult question: What are the criteria for deciding when and how much disorder is warranted, and by how much and what types of injustice?

Recognizing that there is inevitable tension between order and justice in any complex, industrialized and highly urbanized society, we must ask: What degree of injustice will we tolerate to conserve existing order, without which greater injustice may be inevitable? Contrariwise, can there be injustice of such magnitude that no matter what benefits order confers, the preferable alternative would still be the risk of any degree of disorder necessary to act directly against that injustice?

II Regulated Disorder

The market place theory of ideas and the right to freedom of speech and expression [5] illustrate the principles relevant to discovering criteria for the legitimation of direct action within a context of order with justice. The basis for the extraordinary respect paid to free speech and the protection accorded it was summarized in Justice Holmes' famous sentence, when he dissented in *Abrams:* "[T]he best test of truth is the power of thought to get itself accepted in the competition of the market. . . ." [6] In terms of the order-disorder dichotomy, the belief here is that by insuring the machinery for peaceful change with maximum protection there will be less disorder. Peaceful change, or orderly regulatable disorder, requires maximum protection for freedom of speech, because speech, unlike other alternatives, invites the community to respond to the demand for change, in terms of the machinery which is manageable in and by order. Where speech is suppressed, the repression may precipitate decision-making by devices outside the institutionalized structure, resulting in disorder of gross rather than manageable proportions. It would be unwise to deny that the broad protection accorded to speech may intensify the emotional instability which comes from being contained within a political environment able to accommodate attacks upon the ordered structure. But, between instability and the pretense of security existing within a social structure which denies opportunity for public display of alternatives, the accommodation of tolerable disorder will better assure that minimal feeling of security without which there can be no society. Where speech is suppressed in order to minimize the accommodation of change, the sense of security in the stability of the order is illusory, because change is inevitable and an order which fails to accommodate the inevitable invites destruction, not permanence.

The presumption, or perhaps belief (depending upon what one regards as evidence) behind the First Amendment guaranties, is a double one. It is presumed that the viability of order is directly related to its ability to accommodate change,[7] and it is presumed that a democratic order is distinguished from others by the assurance that there will be channels through which people may effectively participate in government at least to the extent of expressing dissatisfaction with what their government is doing. Against this model for order it becomes easy to understand why First Amendment rights are unique, especially when to these presumptions there is added the conviction that from among all the methods by which participation in government is made possible, effective access to the minds of men is the one absolutely essential prerequisite of any system. Granting all this requires virtually absolute protection for freedom of speech.[8] The minds of men may be moved by many different things, including bayonets, but if one believes that a social order which accommodates change need not be intolerably disorderly, then the task is to discover which among the alternatives best accommodate inevitable change.

It will be useful to delineate the scope of direct action as it is used in these contexts. In a way, "direct action" is a euphemism and it might be more accurate, if instead of speaking about the legitimation of direct action, we spoke instead about the legitimation of *resistance*. Where direct action implements order, i.e., where the action carries out values which the stabilized order accommodates, there will be no challenge to the legitimacy of the conduct. The challenge will come only when the direct action also resists values which the stabilized order protects.

Suppose, e.g., the owner of a large manufacturing facility or a great tract of land were to be convinced that he ought to alleviate poverty by distributing the land or the ownership of his plant to the poor in his area; this would constitute direct action. Yet to raise the question as to its legitimacy does violence to the concept with which we are concerned. Giving away that which is yours is action. It may be direct; it may be the most direct action; it may be the most intelligent solution to the problem of poverty which one could devise; but that is not the problem of direct action in terms of its legitimacy, which is our real concern. The reference here to direct action is to action which resists imbedded values, rather than action which seeks to advance or apply such values. Direct action then, is confrontation in which there is explicit rejection and often implicit resistance to an authority which identifies with values contrary to the value of those who take the action.

It may seem anomalous to ask how one legitimates resistance to authority. The question is anything but an anomaly; and on the contrary, the fact that the Constitution does accommodate legitimate resistance to authority is one of its greatest strengths in providing for regulatable disorder. Nor should

39

this be much of a surprise since the Constitution was drafted against the background of 18th century political theory which reflects quite precisely the belief that resistance to governmental power was not only appropriate but even necessary in certain circumstances. There would indeed be an anomaly if the model of constitutional government were that which Austin had in mind when he envisaged the absolute sovereign at the apex of a power structure in which law was the command of that sovereign. Such a view makes it difficult to recognize that the sovereign himself is subject to law or that the people have a residual power to resist sovereign authority. However, the Constitution is a clear rejection of such an Austinian model of sovereignty.

Though there may be no anomaly in the concept of legitimate direct action, even when that entails resistance to authority, this idea does have some paradoxical features. The *Shuttlesworth* case [9] decided in March of 1969, illustrates one such feature. The Reverend Shuttlesworth, after attempting to obtain a permit allegedly necessary in order to hold a parade, demonstration or march within the city of Birmingham, Alabama, did hold such a march even after his efforts to obtain the permit had been frustrated. He was arrested and convicted for violation of the relevant statute and sentenced to 90 days imprisonment at hard labor, with an additional 48 days in default of payment of the fine. Although an Alabama appellate court reversed the conviction, the supreme court of the state sustained the conviction after interpreting the statutory language (under which the permit was to be issued) in such a way that had the statute been drafted that way initially, the conviction might have been valid. The case came before the Supreme Court in the following posture: Shuttlesworth was convicted under a statute which, at the time when he was convicted, had not been interpreted by the supreme court of the state and therefore the language of the statute relevant to his conviction was that contained in the statute itself and not as interpreted. Under that statute, the licensing authorities were given what the Court found to be virtually unbridled freedom to issue the required permit. In holding his parade without the permit required by the statute (which statute had not yet been declared unconstitutional), Shuttlesworth was engaging in direct action, and there was a confrontation in which there was an explicit rejection and an implicit resistance to an authority which identified with values contrary to those held by Shuttlesworth and those who marched with him. There could not have been a clearer case of direct action as I here use that expression. How can one say that there still was legitimate resistance? The Court in reversing the conviction says this: "And our decisions have made clear that a person faced with such an unconstitutional licensing law [as that which faced Shuttlesworth in Birmingham] may ignore it, and engage with impunity in the exercise of the right of free expression for which the law purports to require a license." [10] Perhaps it is worth adding that this was a unanimous decision by the Court with only Justice Marshall taking no part in the decision. The strength of the Court's conclusion (that one may legitimately resist authority) was strengthened by the sentence which followed that which I quoted. There, quoting from a prior decision, the Court added: "The Constitution can hardly be thought to deny to one subjected to the restraints of such an ordinance the right to attack its constitutionality; because he has not yielded to its demands." [11] Could there be a clearer statement of the right—and by that I mean right, not merely liberty—to resist authority? And to speak of a right in this context is to say that what was done was legitimate.

There is another paradoxical feature in the notion of legitimate direct action when that includes resistance to authority. It is especially easy to see this feature in the context of the United States, where there is a federalist system. When the governors of some Southern states after *Brown v. Board of Education* [12] stood on the steps of some local university or public school and said, "No Negro shall enter here," this too was direct action, and in the boldest, clearest, most provocative way. What makes such cases of "official" direct action somewhat paradoxical is just the fact that it is confrontation by authority in which there is explicit rejection and even explicit resistance to another authority which identifies with values contrary to those of the governor who is here acting directly.

When the confrontation is between equally authoritative and institutionalized power structures (e.g., the Supreme Court and a state governor), one would be hard pressed to discover what legitimacy might mean or what might be the procedure for the determination of legitimate resistance in such a context. The attacks on some of the supposed excessively liberal decisions in support of civil rights constitute confrontations of this kind. Here a significant number of states have sought to prevent a different governmental authority, the Supreme Court, from implementing values which the Court regards as imbedded in the existing order. Thus far, such attacks have not been very effective, but there is no question as to the legitimacy of the direct action. This is because the direct action taken by the governors has been to utilize the order itself to frustrate the decisions of the Court. This has been done by passage of deliberately evasive state legislation, by introduction into Congress of legislation aimed at the repression of the Court and by other legitimate, orderly, institutionalized devices, all of which are available to those who have access to the resources for manipulating power. When those with access to institutionalized political power resort to the equivalent of what for the people is direct action, there is revolution or civil war. So the question of legitimacy when a powerful and vested authority resists another such authority is not relevant to us, as we are here concerned only with that more common if not also more provocative problem: What happens when there is resistance to authority by those who do not come clothed in the mantle of vested authority?

How warlike the situation was when the governors and

other state officials sought to directly resist and frustrate integration decrees is shown by the fact that federal troops were required to suppress actual or threatened disorder beyond the degree which was regarded as tolerable. Such cases of governmental resistance to government order are more nearly analogous to the ones relevant here. It is interesting to notice that such direct action—Shall we call it official direct action?—is itself a phenomenon which the Constitution may have intended to accommodate.

The idea of legitimate resistance or orderly disorder despite any paradoxical and even anomalous character may be a central component of that principle which in any non-authoritarian political order is basic, i.e., the rule of law. Under that rule there is the presumption that governmental acts are not legitimate just because they are acts of government. Both the Constitution and the Universal Declaration of Human Rights reflect that presumption by the central place which both accord to conscience and to the priority of the people over the state. In rejecting the fascist theory of state where the people exist for the benefit of the state, the Declaration and the Constitution embrace the rule of law and its presumption as to the status of governmental acts. No modern constitutional democratic society would be possible if one could not legitimately question governmental acts, and hence, when the Supreme Court acts in response to a challenge on the status of some legislation, it is the *Court* which then legitimates that statute.[13] The Court bestows upon the legislation the cloak of legitimacy. Unlike the modern authoritarian versions of the divine right of the kings, pursuant to which legislation comes clothed in legitimacy because of its royal birth, the contrary presumption characterizes a democratic, open, political system in which citizen participation in government is at least accommodated, if not also encouraged.

To recognize that the free, open, economically and socially mobile, liberating, democratic, youthful society presumes not that governmental acts are legitimate just because they are the acts of government inevitably carries with it the presumption that resistance to the acts of government is not necessarily illegitimate. While there is no necessary connection, this presumption strongly supports the need for absolute protection of speech and expression because these are the least disastrous ways of producing change in a manner which can be accommodated within an orderly structure. It is for this reason that I turn now to an examination of the specific accommodation made in the United States to freedom of speech and expression.

III   The Protection of Speech

Many are familiar with the view largely associated with Justice Black that pure speech is protected absolutely by the First Amendment.[14] Less familiar are the positions taken by the other members of the Court who have not subscribed to this absolutist theory. And even more important for direct action is the effect of the First Amendment on the states rather than on the Congress (to which the amendment was directed). According to Justice Black and a minority of the Court, the Fourteenth Amendment absorbed all of the Bill of Rights and therefore everything contained in that Bill is applicable to the states. The majority of the Court, however, has adopted the view that there is a selective incorporation [15] into the Fourteenth Amendment from the Bill, and for these justices, only those rights which they find to be "fundamental" or "required by a sense of justice" are said to have been absorbed into the Fourteenth Amendment.[16] This latter view, which currently dominates the thinking of the Court, entails the complicated task of trying to discover the criteria which determine which rights are fundamental or required by the sense of justice. Our difficulties are increased by asking whether the Bill of Rights exhausts all the basic rights an individual has against the government or whether the Tenth Amendment intends to provide for precisely this case when it states that rights other than those specified in the Constitution are still retained by the people. On such an interpretation, even if all of the Bill is made applicable to the states through the Fourteenth Amendment, there will still be other rights, including the possibility of rights to direct action, which will further limit the possibility of governmental repression. But even if one adopts this latter view, there is still another problem, comparable to that involved when one adopts the selective theory of incorporation from the Bill into the Fourteenth Amendment: namely, where do the standards, the principles, the criteria come from for determining which are the rights guaranteed by the Tenth Amendment in addition to those in the Bill? Does one appeal to fundamental, basic or natural rights, natural justice, natural law, a sense of justice? Where do we discover the principles by which these fundamental matters are settled?

I raise these questions about the Fourteenth and Tenth amendments not so much because the specific content of these two amendments is of interest, but rather because the problem as to their content is quite identical to the problem which one confronts in trying to understand the First Amendment. Once one abandons the absolutist theory of Justice Black, that is, if only some speech is protected by the amendment, where does one discover the criteria by which to determine which speech is protectable? Because even on the absolutist theory of the First Amendment, where there is a distinction made between speech which is absolutely protected and conduct which is not, there is an especially serious question about criteria for legitimacy when the matter concerns direct action other than speech. There is also the further question of whether some expression which is not covered by the First Amendment might still be covered by the Ninth Amendment. Would it make any difference if the criteria by which the meaning of the Tenth Amendment is determined are the same as the criteria cited for determining whether a certain act is protected under the First Amendment?

How does the Supreme Court handle this kind of a problem? Once the Court rejects an absolute theory of protection, as it has for speech as well as conduct, the Court is almost inevitably compelled to proceed on a case by case, ad hoc basis.[17] The disadvantages of such an approach are glaringly apparent. On such a basis, it is almost inevitable that in a conflict between the statutory prohibition which represses speech and freedom for speech, the prohibition will prevail. This is so not only because of the general tendency to favor legislation but also because the Court is unlikely to take on the task involved in striking down the legislation unless the legislative choice was irrational. As in most areas of constitutional litigation (although admittedly less so in free speech), the Court has time and again indicated that where the legislative choice is rational, almost total deference must be paid to it. Just what "rational" means in this context is not wholly clear, but it would appear to mean that the choice made by the legislature at the very least helps achieve a goal which is socially desirable. Since it is almost always possible to give importance to such goals as the regulation does serve, the likelihood of declaring the regulation unconstitutional, despite a restriction on free speech, becomes rather remote.

Thus, when the Court proceeds on an ad hoc basis, it will be weighing the competing interests to see which ought to prevail.[18] This interest-weighing approach is familiar enough in other areas of constitutional litigation, and perhaps almost by reason of its general utility in other areas rather than because it belongs here, interest-weighing has come to be utilized by the Court in the free speech area, although one may seriously question its appropriateness here. Nevertheless, it is reasonably clear that the Court now relies upon an interest-weighing approach, and this has been so at least since 1950 when the Court decided *Douds* and rather clearly rejected an absolutist theory for any First Amendment rights.[19] A number of the justices, in writing opinions since that time, at least until the *New York Times* [20] case, have specifically spoken of the open and frank weighing of competing interests as the proper judicial process for deciding which speech is free and which is not.[21]

Although those whose speech was repressed may not agree, it did not take long for the Court to realize, after rejecting *Douds,* that an ad hoc approach to First Amendment rights would largely defeat the underlying premise about the "market place for ideas" which warranted the extreme protection for speech.[22] Where the Court approaches a matter so fundamental as speech on an ad hoc basis, it is almost inevitable that the speech which most requires protection, i.e., the speech which is most unpopular is also most likely to be the object of prosecutorial zeal under repressive state legislation. It is also clear that where the Court does not have a clear standard for protection but approaches cases on an ad hoc basis, only those speakers who are well-funded or very brave will enter the market place when the risk they take for exposing their ideas is incarceration, or a long drawnout, costly court battle to prevent it. But even if these objections were not enough, it should be clear that an ad hoc interest-weighing approach to free speech certainly diminishes the vitality of the protection for speech, and may even destroy the underlying premise about citizen participation in government.

Aware of the restrictions on free speech which an ad hoc approach to the speech cases could produce, at least since 1964 when the Court decided *New York Times v. Sullivan,* the Court may now be trying to move away from this approach. Instead, it is trying to forge a principle for speech protection which would rely upon some definitional criteria to which one could appeal for determining in advance whether or not speech is protected under the First Amendment.[23] The *New York Times* case was not a general free speech case, but rather one questioning whether criticism of a certain government official would

47

be libel. With this case, by placing the burden on the official claiming the libel, the Court much encouraged the possibility for criticism of officials.[24] In two recent cases, one involving General Walker, the Court expanded the protection afforded by the *Times* case to include persons who, even if not public officials, would still have the burden of showing the libel because they were public figures.[25] Now, at least for protection from libel, if an individual, even if not a public official, enters the market place of ideas by speaking out, he may not complain of libel if, as a result of speech by another which is neither deliberately nor maliciously false, he is criticized or attacked. This is part of a "seller beware" theory of free speech: if you enter the foray of the market place, you and your ideas become fair game because it is more important to keep the market free and open than to protect you from libel. Justice Douglas, in fact, would seem to go further. He appears to suggest that rather than a public-figures test, the question should be only whether the speech is directed to a public issue.[26] Under such a test, the abandonment of absolute protection to speech would not be very serious since all speech which is concerned with a public issue would qualify at least regarding protection from libel prosecution.

The diminished risk of libel is hardly the only problem confronting those concerned with the expansive reading of First Amendment privileges for speech and expression, but the libel cases are suggestive and help in articulating a theory for the substitution of an absolute protection, if that need be abandoned.

For persons involved in civil rights direct-action demonstrations, protection from prosecution for libel is probably not very significant. Persons involved in such demonstrations are likely to be concerned with incarceration, not libel. The real problem arises with regard to statutory schemes which attempt to restrain the expression of opinion contrary to the prevailing values. However, the libel cases are instructive in suggesting that the Court now appreciates the inadequacy of an ad hoc interest-weighing approach when dealing with First Amendment rights, because there may be overriding interests which demand a kind of protection not available on the ad hoc approach. It is the recognition of the thesis that these rights are different from those elsewhere protected even in the Constitution.

Perhaps in the area of economic regulation, an interest-weighing approach is adequate. If a community wishes to rezone an area in a way which is disadvantageous to a private property owner, one may understand the justification of such legislation or regulations where, on balance, a higher social purpose prevails over the private loss. But where speech is involved, may it not be that the cost in terms of repression is always too high unless one finds some socially useful purpose which goes beyond that of keeping the channels of government open, viable and free so that the democratic process of change is implemented, thereby avoiding the likelihood of change through violent disorder? Unlike other areas of constitutional litigation (where the Court shows a constant unwillingness to disturb the legislative scheme if there is found some socially appropriate purpose served by that scheme) in the area of free speech the Court should rather adopt what one writer has called the "least intrusive alternative." [27] That is, sustain the legislation only if there is not some other legislative scheme which will serve the socially useful purpose while not restricting free speech as much as the legislation proposed. On such a theory, the legislative choice prevails unless there is a less intrusive alternative which is clearly less restrictive, and still within the range of effectiveness and cost comparable to that of the legislation actually proposed.

While it must be admitted that such an approach to the free speech problems has not been pursued by the Court, the recent libel cases indicate a willingness by the Court to reexamine the principles of decision-making (not of the criteria,

49

per se) for these cases. Out of such reexamination, there may emerge a new approach to the problems of free speech, which, while not going as far as Black's absolutist theory, will no longer compel litigants to endure years of trial litigation in order to discover retroactively, whether their speech was free and protected. That the Court recognizes the advantages of something like the less intrusive alternative is suggested by the line of decision from 1961 to 1965 where the Court ruled on over 30 trespass or breach-of-peace sit-in cases and in nearly all of which the demonstrators prevailed.[28] However, by reversing the convictions on very narrow, restrictive grounds, the Court avoided reaching the basic constitutional questions. The effect of these decisions was to encourage sit-in demonstrations by reversing the convictions on these technical grounds. For example, in *Bain v. The City of Columbia*,[29] the Court reversed the trespass conviction on the grounds that the statute failed explicitly to outlaw a refusal to leave the premises. The effect of such a line of decisions, I submit, is to show that while legislation restricting expression, of which a sit-in can be an instance, may be tolerable, legislation must be drafted so as to prevent the harm while still making the least intrusive restriction upon the right which is constitutionally protected. Perhaps the argument could be put this way: The higher in the constitutional scheme of values, the more justification there need be for repression, the more ingenious and imaginative the legislature must be to find that statutory scheme which achieves the minimum amount of repression compatible with those goals considered sufficiently important to warrant the repression.

In this connection, *Gregory v. The City of Chicago* [30] is exceptionally interesting. Here the Court reversed the disorderly conduct conviction of Dick Gregory which arose out of a widely publicized incident. The case grew out of the march arranged by Mr. Gregory to demand the discharge of the superintendent of Chicago schools who was alleged to have acted too slowly to end segregation practices in the schools. The marchers walked quietly around the block on which Mayor Daley's house is located. They were extremely orderly and at no time did they engage in anything which could have been regarded as disorderly. On the contrary, even when pelted by tomatoes and eggs, the marchers did maintain complete discipline, under direction from Mr. Gregory, and none attempted any physical reaction even under abuse. The evidence from Gregory as well as others shows that the police did try to protect them and tried to apprehend those who improperly disturbed the marchers. But at a certain point, when a sufficiently large crowd gathered, estimated at from 1200 to 2,000 people who threatened the marchers with serious physical injury, even death, the police asked Gregory and the other marchers to disband. When they refused to do so, they were arrested on the disorderly conduct charge.

In an extremely short opinion of less than one page, the Chief Justice, speaking for the Court, reversed the convictions on the ground that they had been indicted under a statute which did not include the refusal to obey a police officer as an instance of disorderly conduct. They had been charged and convicted for holding a demonstration not for refusal to obey the police and consequently since the basis of the conviction was contrary to First Amendment protections, the conviction was reversed. Despite the highly technical character of this basis for reversal, Justice Douglas concurred in the Court's opinion.

Commenting on his case, Gregory is reported as having said this:

> Every once in awhile, the check and balance system of our Constitutional government really comes on strong. It is always heartening to black folks to see the Supreme Court overrule federal agencies, as well as state and local courts, which have misused their authority to suppress the rights of decent thinking folks.
>
> Of course I never did like to use the term "Supreme Court" to refer to that august body of legal minds. I like to think of them as our "alternate sponsors." And it makes sense, when you think about

it. The men in the white sheets took our rights away from us; it's only proper that the men in the black robes should give them back.[31]

There was a separate concurrence by Justice Black, joined by Justice Douglas, which is of particular interest on the question of least intrusive alternatives. In this concurrence, Justice Black, whose views are particularly interesting because of his defense of the absolute protection which ought be accorded speech, states that it is becoming increasingly clear that "when groups with diametrically opposed, deep seated views are permitted to air the promotional grievances, side by side, on city streets, tranquility and order cannot be maintained even by the joint efforts of the finest and best officers and of those who desire to be the most law-abiding protestors of their grievances." He also points out that "the Constitution does not bar enactment of laws regulating conduct, even though connected with speech, press, assembly, and petition, if such laws specifically bar only the conduct deemed obnoxious and are carefully and narrowly aimed at that forbidden conduct." He then adds what is particularly interesting here: "the dilemma revealed by this record is a crying example of a need for some narrowly drawn law." [32] Thus, Justice Black, without stating what such law might be or how narrowly it need be drawn, is rather clearly supporting the theory of the least intrusive alternative in the area of free speech. If speech may not be protected absolutely at least it must be protected to the degree where the repression which is condoned is no greater than that needed to satisfy some legitimate social purpose which warrants the repression. The legitimate social purpose which Black apparently envisaged in this situation was the protection of protesters as well as the protection of the right of people to peacefully reside in their homes without being subjected to political demonstrations at certain times or places. Under such a view, legislation restrictive of free speech becomes tolerated on the general theory that among the socially important goals of government (in addition to that of providing access to the market place of ideas) is the goal that the market place shall not be so congested by traffic, speech or otherwise, that it becomes unmanageable. On such a theory as this, requirements for permits in order to stage demonstrations may become acceptable when the basis for the grant of a permit is in no way contingent upon the character or the content of the protest so long as it does not, e.g., interfere with the proper free flow of traffic or otherwise prevent the utilization of a common resource by other persons whose interests are equally legitimate.

Even if the Court were to articulate some further definitional criteria for tolerable repressive legislation, it would not mean the end to the ad hoc approach to free speech cases. So long as absolute protection is not accorded there will continually be the need for case by case review. For example, under the test suggested above, that of the least intrusive alternative, there is still much the same disadvantage which characterized Justice Holmes' clear and present danger test for determining the permissible content of speech. With this difference however: The clear and present danger test, although often misunderstood, was designed to determine the permissible content of free speech, not to determine whether speech could be regulated in some specific way. Nor was it designed to deal with the problem of repressive legislation, except as that legislation was directed to content. It may be that with the virtual death of the obscenity barrier to speech,[33] the problem of content is unlikely to be the one which will require much judicial or even legislative attention. Any speech which is concerned with public issues, particularly in light of the most recent libel cases, is probably protected as to content. The only limitation would seem to be that of the libel cases; i.e., there may not be malicious or deliberate falsehood. If, then, clear and present danger is no longer likely to be a barrier to what one may say, the more enduring questions are likely to concern how, when or where it may be said. In this connection the problem of legislation will continue to be the critical impediment to unrestricted free speech, and on this question, the least intrusive alternative may be preferable.

In other words, the clear and present danger test cannot be used to determine the how, when and where; it can be used to determine permissible content; but content, I am suggesting, is no longer the dynamic aspect of the free speech problem. If then, a case by case method is incapable of determining whether the legislative scheme is the least repressive method compatible with the overriding demand for protected speech, how is this any improvement on the ad hoc approach? I suggest that where the Court once sustains legislation because it is drafted with sufficient precision and narrowly enough so that it is the least intrusive legislative scheme, it does then lay down predictable guidelines for the manner of expression, which, when coupled with the virtual demise of conditions on content, would leave speech considerably freer than it has been under the decisions of the past. Although the past decisions, particularly since 1961, almost always sustained the right of expression, they have still required long judicial battles, expenditure of much money and great risk to persons, whereas under the least intrusive test for legislation, which regulates mode and manner and in view of the demise of the contents requirement, expression would be considerably less impeded.

There is perhaps an even less restrictive approach to the what, how, when, and where questions on freedom of expression than the least intrusive test for repressive legislation. Under this test, which possibly goes furthest towards the goal of absolute protection while not quite reaching that position, the content of speech as well as the manner, time and place of delivery would be subject to restriction under legislation which impowers the proper officials (usually the police) to act only when they are unable to prevent by other means the real, present danger of riot or other illegal conduct. That is, under this test the expression would always be free unless it could be shown that it would incite to riot if not suppressed.

Although much weakened by the later decision in *Edwards*,[34] the Court's decision in *Feiner* [35] did sustain the conviction of a speaker who urged Negroes to take violent action against white people. However, from 1962 to 1966 (during the rise of the civil rights cases), this case was largely ignored, but it may now return as the compromise position between the absolutists and the ad hoc definitionalists.

It is perhaps useful to know that a decision like *Feiner*, which sustained the restriction on the inflammatory speech, is directed not to the content of what the speaker was saying but rather to the method, time and place of expression. It is a special application of clear and present danger criteria not for the suppression of ideas which are thought dangerous but for the suppression because the time, place or circumstances make the expression a clear and present danger. However, contrast with *Feiner*, the statement of the Court in *Brown v. Louisiana*, decided in 1966: "Participants in an orderly demonstration in a public place are not chargeable with the danger, unprovoked except by the fact of the constitutionally protected demonstration itself, that their critics might react with disorder or violence." [36] Although this statement would seem to suggest that audience reaction to speech which is protected is not a criterion for suppression, the *Feiner* decision still stands, and because it could so easily have been overruled in this case or later cases, I am led to believe that there is still vitality in *Feiner*. In view of the most recent decisions stressing as they do the Court's abhorrence of violence, it is quite possible that the *Feiner* limitation on free speech may be the one on which the Court will ultimately settle until the demand for absolute protection compels abandonment of even this condition. Despite the plausibility of a *Feiner* limitation on speech, I shall try to show why it, too, is unattractive.

Rather than attempt to predict Supreme Court decisions,

I shall concentrate on the issues in terms of the values which are protected by alternative decision-making approaches and criteria. It is worth noticing that the incite-to-riot test is objectionable if it suggests that speech which is effective enough to incite is not protected, while speech which is ineffective or aims only at informing, illustrating, or clarifying, is protected. It is useful to remember that Eugene Debs received over 900,000 votes for President of the United States while in prison after a unanimous Court sustained his conviction for attempting to incite men not to serve in the armed forces and for attempting to induce insubordination among those who did serve. To suggest that these 900,000 people are outside the scope of the market place of ideas is to offer a new theory of democracy which hardly commends itself as obviously desirable.

If an absolute free speech protection cannot be accorded, the potential violence of hostile spectators ought not to be the criterion which determines whether or not a speaker may be suppressed.[37] In *Wright v. Georgia* [38] and *Barr v. City of Columbia*,[39] the Court does seem to support the view that the potential audience hostility should not be a criterion for determining suppression. The Court has not yet gone so far as to say that a state may only move against a potentially hostile audience when a peaceful speaker is incendiary.[40] The issue, however, is more subtle. If all the First Amendment protects is speech which explains, discusses, comments upon, analyzes or clarifies but does not provoke, then the amendment has been stripped of its vitality in terms of the market place of ideas. If to this restrictive reading of the amendment there is added the fact that access to the effective means of communication are seldom within the control of those who need the First Amendment protection, there is left an amendment totally ineffective for protecting the market place of ideas theory. A *Feiner* type reading of the First Amendment makes a shambles of the basic democratic ideal of permitting, if not encouraging, citizen participation in government.

To suppress speech because of the possibility that the audience may commit acts which are crimes is to say that when the fire marshall knowingly permits oily rags to accumulate in a public building, the smoker whose cigarette ignites those rags is alone responsible for the deaths which ensue when there is a fire. Between the careless smoker and the fire marshall charged with the responsibility for the prevention of fire hazards, I should prefer to see the fire marshall punished if punishment need be meted out at all. In this analogy to the speech situation, when a speaker gives an oration whose content is privileged but which, because of the time, place or circumstances may be incendiary, then one could hardly maintain that the situation is inflammatory only because of the time or circumstances. Rather, it must be that such conditions already obtain in that community so that this further element, this cigarette ash, incites passions already at the kindling point. In a community of happy, contented people, it is unlikely that any speech which is not deliberately or maliciously false would incite to riot.

If in an inflammatory situation the most powerful force for the prevention and control of that situation, the government, fails to act to relieve those conditions which make the situation inflammatory, is not this itself a contribution to the circumstances? If the prevention of riots is serious enough to warrant suppression of speech, then it ought to be at least serious enough to warrant governmental action to alleviate conditions which drive men to inflammatory speech. Between a government sufficiently careless or even worse, sufficiently indifferent, to permit conditions which make a mere act of speech so inflammatory as to cause a riot, and the speaker who was exercising a constitutionally protected freedom, it should require much more than a presumption in favor of police helplessness to prevent riot other than by suppression of the speech or even other forms of expression, before the repressive action is condoned. After all, it surely need be recognized that the legislature which authorized and the police who implement the suppression of speech have, if not a monopoly, a large enough concentration of power and authority to prevent conditions which breed riot.

I have deliberately used the ambiguous expression "conditions which breed riot," because two kinds of conditions are relevant. First, there are social conditions, such as poverty, injustice, inequality, alienation, disenfranchisement, frustration, etc., which may be the conditions against which the speaker is rallying. Second, and perhaps more concretely, the same legislature which enacts repressive legislation also has a monopoly on the legitimate force for the prevention of riots. If a speaker is likely to be incendiary, then let there be enough police allocated to prevent the riot. If the situation becomes incendiary when there are not enough police, as was the case in *Feiner* and in *Gregory,* and if more police cannot be had in time, then perhaps legislation need be drafted which anticipates an extraordinary situation. Maybe what ought to be permitted in terms of a least intrusive alternative is legislation pursuant to which a speaker or demonstrator must comply with the order of a police officer to cease when there is the danger of a serious riot; but then the state must guarantee an appropriate and effective forum to the speaker or demonstrator which will give him access to the audience he wishes to reach. An appropriate forum would include one where the state can exercise or display such force as may be necessary to prevent that which is illegal.

In suggesting it may be the state's duty to provide access to an appropriate forum when the state has seen fit to repress speech or expression which would otherwise be free, I am not unmindful of the practical problems involved. Since access to the media of mass communication may be more crucial than the sometimes overly academic debates about freedom of speech, it seems to me that the practical problems are manageable so long as the state will supply access to the mass media. It is largely the need for access to mass media which has helped generate much of the new wave in the area of First Amendment developments, i.e., conduct rather than speech where the conduct is expressed in a deliberately provocative way so that the media will pay attention.

It is worth noticing that the distinction between speech which is protected and conduct which is not protected by the First Amendment because it is not pure speech is artificial in many important respects.[41] If the First Amendment is designed to protect the right to speak freely, it could not have been intended to cover only the case of a man who whispers to his wife in the privacy of their bed chamber. If there is a right to free speech, it must certainly include the right to speak in a way which will be heard. It may include the right to amplify one's voice [42] and the right to an area where there is an audience which the speaker wishes to reach. If these aspects of conduct are not included within the protection of free speech, it is difficult to understand what the First Amendment is about. If the drafters of the Constitution were concerned only with privacy in the bed chamber, they did not need to include the First Amendment. That amendment was designed to encourage and implement a theory about tolerable, regulatable disorder; but if the amendment is circumscribed so that only bed chamber speech is left free, then the purpose of the amendment has been defeated.

If the purpose of making the speech-conduct distinction is that pure speech is absolutely protected but the way in which one speaks, or the place, or the method, or the mode of expression is subject to restraint, then the distinction would seem to be hardly the best way of solving the problem. The interest to be secured, viz., the prevention of riots, may in some cases warrant restriction on speech and in other cases, restriction on conduct. One could say perfectly innocent, unprovocative things which in no way endanger the interests of order but in a way or at a place or at a time which makes the entire situation a threat. On the other hand, one may say highly provocative things in a peaceful, calm, quiet way so that there is little threat to peace and order. Similarly, there may be conduct which is threatening because of what it expresses and conduct which is threatening because of the time, place or mode of expression despite the relatively unprovocative content of the message. If, therefore, the justification for less freedom for conduct as expression is the preservation of interests sufficiently important even when confronted by the demand for freedom of speech and ideas, it would seem that a recognition of those interests in juxtaposition to the demand for freedom should be the basis for decision, rather than the artificial distinction between speech and conduct.

Even with the use of the speech-conduct distinction, it is necessary to recognize that merely because a man's mouth is moving and sounds come forth, it does not follow that there is speech which is protected under the First Amendment. Likewise, merely because one is acting in connection with a public issue, it does not follow that there is conduct which qualifies for First Amendment protection. Recognizing then, that First Amendment protection, no matter how widely interpreted, will require some distinctions to be drawn between cases of speech and conduct which are protected and those which are not, it may be useful to consider how a line may be drawn, if not between marginal cases, at least between paradigm cases. If one adopts an absolutist interpretation of the protection accorded pure speech, he is likely to maintain a sharp distinction between speech and conduct. Contrariwise, the less absolute the protection of pure speech, the less necessary is a sharp speech-conduct distinction. But in either event, overt conduct which is criminal does not become converted into protected expression because it is directed at the expression of an idea, which idea, if communicated verbally, would have received First Amendment protection. As Professor Thomas Emerson, one of the most astute commentators on the amendment, has said:

> Expression often takes place in a context of action, or is closely linked with it, or is equivalent in its impact. In these mixed cases, it is necessary to decide, however artificial the distinction may ap-

pear to be, whether the conduct be classified as one or the other. This judgment must be guided by consideration of whether the conduct partakes of the essential qualities of expression or action.[43]

Perhaps wisely, the Court has as yet not undertaken the task of trying to lay down criteria for the decision on which conduct has communicative value and which should therefore get First Amendment protection. Instead, the Court has again proceeded on an ad hoc basis weighing the alleged evils of the conduct against the alleged social values to be achieved by suppression. This does not mean that the Court does not sustain conduct which is unaccompanied by speech, for in a number of cases, the contrary has been held. Thus, as Justice Fortas said for the Court in *Brown v. Louisiana:* ". . . [T]his Court has repeatedly stated, these [First Amendment] rights are not confined to verbal expression. They embrace appropriate types of action which certainly include the right in a peaceable and orderly manner to protest by silent and reproachful presence. . . ." [44] Even in some of the earlier cases involving sit-ins, staged in connection with the contemporary civil rights movement, the Court recognized that a sit-in was a form of communication and as such protected under the amendment.[45]

Even more suggestive in this context have been cases in which the Court has considered the use of a flag as a device for communicating and expressing. In *Stromberg,* the defendant displayed a red flag in order to express his opposition to certain established interests and was prosecuted under a state statute which prohibited such a display. The Court reversed on the basis of the First Amendment because that display of the flag was a form of speech. Writing for the Court, Justice Jackson said specifically: ". . . The flag salute is a form of utterance. Symbolism is a primitive but effective way of communicating ideas." [46] And it was an earlier flag salute case, *Barnett,*[47] which probably more than any other case firmly established the principle that communicating conduct may deserve protection under the First Amendment even when not accompanied by

61

speech. In *Barnett,* the Court decided that it was an unconstitutional restriction of freedom of speech and religion to require school children to salute a flag. That case also involved the recitation of the Pledge of Allegiance, but the language of the decision strongly supports the view that even the salute by itself would have been an unconstitutional abridgement of freedom of speech and religion.

In view of *Stromberg* and *Barnett,* which so clearly recognized that display of or salute to a flag is the functional equivalent of protected free speech, it is interesting to observe that although all states have statutes prohibiting the desecration of the flag, no court decision has held such statutes to be contrary to the First Amendment. Yet it is difficult to see any significant distinction between compulsory salute to a flag or display of a flag or destruction of a flag in terms of the communicative equivalent of speech.[48] Displaying, saluting or destroying are differentiable in terms of the message communicated, but not on the question of whether there is communication. There may, of course, be other considerations. One might think that destroying a flag is like incendiary speech, for it might well be that displaying the flag of South Africa to a group of Negroes demonstrating in support of civil rights would be more provocative and incendiary than destroying the American flag before the same audience.[49] Yet in the most important case thus far to have gone through the courts, a case decided by the highest court in New York, the defendant was found guilty under a statute which prohibits public mutilation of the flag.[50] The court recognized the possibility of protected conduct under the First Amendment but found that burning the flag constituted a clear and present danger that the public peace would be disrupted. While this decision is interesting, it does indicate a lack of appreciation for the meaning of the clear and present danger test, which was not designed to determine the repressibility of conduct but rather to provide a decisional criterion for suppressing speech because of its content. But this court, like other courts which have considered desecration cases, did not undertake any examination of the real public interests which were at stake.

Against the background of *Stromberg* and *Barnett*, the decision of the Court in *O'Brien* is of exceptional interest. In *O'Brien*, the defendant was prosecuted for burning his draft card. Seven members of the Court sustained the conviction, and Chief Justice Warren, writing for majority, said:

> We cannot accept the view that an apparently limitless variety of conduct can be labeled "speech" whenever the person engaged in the conduct intends thereby to express an idea. . . . This Court has held that when "speech" and "non-speech" elements are combined in the same course of conduct, a sufficiently important governmental interest in regulating the non-speech element can justify incidental limitations on First Amendment freedoms.[51]

The "sufficiently important governmental interest" which warranted the conviction under the repressive statute relevant here, was the necessary administration of the Selective Service machinery. The socially useful purpose at which the sustained, but repressive congressional enactment was aimed, was found in the legitimate Selective Service requirement that an individual have in his possession a draft card. Yet it is difficult to resist the conclusion that the prohibition upon burning a draft card added little to the administration of the draft system since failure to have a draft card in one's possession was already punishable under existing legislation. Consequently, the specific identification for punishment of draft-card burning after that kind of conduct evolved as a method for expressing antiwar sentiments, could hardly be regarded as anything other than congressional expression of disdain for those prepared to attack American involvement in Vietnam.

In *O'Brien* it is clear that the Court's rejection of the First Amendment argument was made after a balancing act in which the interest of the government in the administration of a draft law was balanced against the interest in free speech. Although there is probably some expressive conduct sufficiently inimical to the draft law to warrant repressive legislation, in *O'Brien,* the Court made no effort at identifying the real issues or the real values which were to be preserved, protected or repressed.[52] Even if only an ad hoc approach is feasible, this kind of deference to repressive legislation merely because it is legislation is contrary to the very meaning of the First Amendment freedoms. It would be bad enough to recognize that there is no way to deal with these cases other than on an ad hoc basis, but to add to this the theory that legislation comes shielded by an overwhelming presumption of validity so that the Court will not even examine into the question of whether there is a socially useful purpose served, let alone whether that purpose could be served by less repressive legislation, then the First Amendment has indeed been struck from its "preferred position."

That Congress did improperly single out a specific form of expression for punishment and that the Court did sanction this in *O'Brien* is suggested by the fact that neither Congress nor the Selective Service have seen fit to attack directly by either legislation or by systematic enforcement under existing regulations the thousands of cases in which men have sent their draft cards back. In these cases there is a violation of existing regulation in that the individual does not have a card in his possession. The point here is that so far as regards the distinction between expression by speech and expression by conduct in burning one's draft card or in turning it in is, the acts of burning or returning the card are functionally equivalent expressions. If there is any violation, it is the violation of the prohibition against failing to have a draft card in one's possession. Whether or not the failure is due to the intentional burning or the intentional turning in or due to any other deliberate act, the only punishable aspect of the situation is the failure to possess a card. The failure of Congress to specifically deal with the deliberate return of the draft card while dealing with the burning of the card, reveals that Congress was concentrating upon the expressive component in the act and not upon the component which was concerned with facilitation of the draft system, that is, failing to have a card in one's possession.

Perhaps *O'Brien* is explained by the fact that the Court was reacting to the escalating violence which had become a part of the anti-Vietnam demonstration movement. Such a pragmatic, unprincipled, dynamic rather than rational explanation or even justification for a decision of the Court is unwelcome. One likes to think that the exigencies of the moment are not reflected by a body insulated from the pressures of the kind to which a legislature is expected to respond. What in large part distinguishes a judicial tribunal from a legislative body is its commitment to the long range community goals rather than its responsiveness to the exigencies of a particular occasion. When a Court functions like a legislature in its response to the crises of the moment instead of committing itself endurably to the long-range values of the kind of society which it is hoped we will have, then we can expect that the Court will cease to receive that kind of community respect which is necessary for the judicial process to function effectively.

When the community ceases to support the Court because it does not find the Court acting as a court but rather performing functions which in our vision of power are expected of other parts of government, the consequences for long-range community values are likely to be even more disastrous than the temporary abandonment of those values by the Court in any particular decision. Yet, one would have to be politically more dead than alive not to see that there is much need to recognize that the line between the functions of government sometimes becomes blurred indeed. Some argue very persuasively that the Court ought to be responsive to the crises of society, and that when the legislature fails to alleviate some conditions which are exceptionally intolerable under long-range community values which the Constitution expresses, then

65

it is proper for the Court to be not only corrective, but creative.

This is not the place [53] to examine the contemporary controversy about neutral principles of Constitution decision making as opposed to what Martin Shapiro has called "political jurisprudence." [54] It seems to me that *O'Brien* was wrongly decided. Under the conservative theory of neutral principles, it was wrongly decided because the Court sustained repressive congressional legislation which was antithetical to long-range community values, which are embodied, indeed enshrined, in a long line of decisions. On the other hand, under a theory which favors greater judicial creativity, it is hard to understand how the Court could have suppressed the act in *O'Brien*, even if there had been some greater showing that draft card burning was a serious impediment to the enforcement of the Selective Service system.

It is worth recalling that in the sit-in cases, the Court generally recognized the expressive quality of a sit-in and protected it under the First Amendment. Similarly in the flag salute and display cases, the Court did recognize the expressive component of the acts and sustained the expression over statutory schemes for regulation. Contrasted with these two areas where the First Amendment prevailed over repressive statutory schemes is *O'Brien*, where the expressive component of the conduct involving protests against the war in Vietnam did not prevail.

The last area I shall consider before trying to find a general theory for distinguishing expressive conduct and speech, concerns the cases involving picketing. While picketing may be entitled to separate protection under the guarantees for freedom of assembly or petition or both,[55] whether the free speech rights would anyway have required the protection is rather a different question. Unlike a sit-in where the Court has pointed out that the act itself communicates because the sit-in is now so well recognized in the community,[56] picketing without a sign does not in and of itself, constitute a clear expression of some particular view.[57] Perhaps this less communicative quality of picketing helps explain the view of the Court in the first *Cox* case where the majority stated that the First Amendment does not afford the same protection to ". . . those who communicate by conduct such as patrolling, marching, and picketing . . . as [it would] afford to those who communicate ideas by pure speech." [58] Demonstrations by way of picketing or sit-ins are particularly interesting in trying to discover the criteria to which the Court has appealed for legitimating direct action. For it was not until *Adderley* [59] was decided in 1966 that the Court did uphold the conviction of participants in a peaceful civil rights demonstration.

Although First Amendment rights have prevailed over repressive legislation which would prohibit or improperly limit access to a public park, public streets, the ground outside the state capitol or the city hall, it does not follow that there is unlimited access to these places for the expression of ideas even when relevant to a public issue.[60] On the contrary, the Court has recognized that a state may reasonably restrict public places by nondiscriminatory rules.[61] From the earliest civil rights sit-in cases up to *Adderley,* the Court consistently sustained peaceful sit-ins. Even in *Brown v. Louisiana,* decided in the same year as *Adderley,* in a five to four decision, the Court reversed a breach of peace conviction of Negro civil rights demonstrators who staged a Saturday morning sit-in at a library after forewarning the local sheriff. All admitted the purpose was to protest segregation generally rather than some inequity of the library. No opinion in this case won five votes and there was an articulate dissent by Justices Black, Clark, Harlan and Stewart, who were impressed by the fact that the sit-in was staged inside a public building rather than on a street, in a park, in front of the city hall or on the grounds of the state capitol building. They were impressed by the fact that "a public library [is] a place dedicated to quiet, to knowledge, and to beauty." [62] In the same year, *Adderley* was decided by five to four voting the other

67

way. There some students were convicted of demonstrating at the county jail where they were protesting the arrest and incarceration of fellow students held in that building. The demonstration was on the jail grounds. The Court, speaking through Justice Black, found that the state statute prohibiting this kind of trespass was sufficiently specific and that it was within the power of the state to preserve the property under its control for its lawfully dedicated purpose and that the demonstration did interfere with the use of the building as intended.

For reasons quite comparable to those which lead me to find the *O'Brien* case wrongly decided, I also think the decision in *Adderley* was wrong. Even if the Court need proceed on an ad hoc basis and does not adopt more nearly absolute protection for freedom of speech and expression, in both *O'Brien* and *Adderley* the interest-weighing approach which the Court does use seems to me to have taken inadequate account of the meaning of the First Amendment as contrasted to the repressive legislation as applied in these cases. In *O'Brien,* the legislation was clearly repressive and aimed at precisely the kind of conduct involved in the case which came before the Court. In *Adderley,* it was the application of the legislation to the facts of that case which made the statute objectionable. That the Court itself was unhappy about *Adderley* is suggested by the decision two years later in *Logan Valley.*[63] In *Adderley,* the Court said: "The State, no less than a private owner of property, has power to preserve the property under its control for the use to which it is lawfully dedicated." [64] On this basis as well as for other reasons, the Court found that the demonstration at the jail interfered with the use for which the property was dedicated and therefore the demonstration was illegitimate even though peaceful. In *Logan Valley,* on the contrary, the Court sustained the right of a labor organization's picketing march on the privately owned grounds of a shopping center and by six to three held that the First Amendment protected this picketing. The shopping center was said to be "functionally equivalent

68

to a [municipal] 'business block.' " [65] Here the question was whether the private owner displaced a public function, i.e., shopping centers replaced the public downtown areas which in prior cases had been held to be appropriate for picketing demonstrations in support of labor organization objectives. Thus *Logan Valley* strongly suggests the view that the legitimacy of a demonstration, at least as regards the place for demonstrations, may depend upon its appropriateness.[66] In *Logan Valley,* even though the property was private and not dedicated public property, the labor picketing was at the most appropriate place. Had the organizing pickets been compelled to go elsewhere, how could they have communicated their message to the audience they wished to reach, namely, those who use the shopping center? What more appropriate place was there for their picketing than at the shopping center even though it was private? Applying *Logan Valley* to the general problem of *Adderley*, it seems to me to reinforce the conclusion I suggest. *Adderley* was wrongly decided. As in *O'Brien,* it gave excessive and unwarranted weight to an administrative interest of the state and thereby suppressed the public interest in having adequate and even appropriate demonstrations in connection with public issues. What place was more appropriate than the jail to protest the incarceration of students arrested and placed within that jail? [67]

In my view, therefore, *Adderley* was wrong for three different reasons. First, because the Court opened a Pandora's box in using proximity criteria to determine the legitimacy of a peaceful demonstration. When will a demonstration be illegitimate because it is too close to a jail? How close is too close? When is a demonstration on jail grounds? The distinctions on such criteria are much too narrow to compel people to risk incarceration or the loss of an important right, indeed a right possibly more important than any other in our constitutional scheme, the right to freedom of expression. Second, the decision is wrong because even if the Court need adopt an ad hoc bal-

ancing approach there were no sufficiently important administrative interests on the part of the state to warrant the
suppression of the First Amendment rights; there was no overwhelmingly important social purpose served by application of
the legislation. In this respect, *O'Brien* was even more objectionable, but *Adderley* was bad enough in that trivial, and
probably inconsequential, inconveniences to the prison administration were made sufficient grounds for suppression of a
peaceful demonstration otherwise protectable under the amendment. There is nothing in the case or record to show that the
demonstration did in any significant way interfere with the use
of the prison or the function and administration of that facility.
Third, *Adderley* is wrong because a peaceful demonstration at
an appropriate private place ought not be suppressed even
when significant governmental interests allegedly serving a
socially useful purpose are frustrated by that demonstration.
If the contrary position is taken, it must mean that the social
purposes served by the repressive legislation are even more important than those purposes which lie behind the rights protected by the First Amendment. Nothing done in a prison can
be said to be more important than the protection of First
Amendment rights to speech and expression. What if, contrary
to the actual facts of *Adderley,* the demonstration did interfere
with the delivery of some food to the prison or even with the
delivery of some prisoners to that prison. Why should that
slight inconvenience which could hardly be said to cause any
serious administrative problems to the prison, be thought
enough to warrant the suppression of that peaceful demonstration? Perhaps, if it could be shown that the demonstration,
contrary to the facts on record in *Adderley,* was likely to
produce an uncontrollable prison riot, one might conceive of
the necessity to suppress the demonstration or move it to an
area outside of the prison grounds. But where the worst that
could happen is that the demonstration would temporarily
inconvenience the performance of some prison function, then

it hardly seems appropriate to say that just because the demonstration is at the most appropriate place that therefore the demonstration is suppressible. In this respect, it is even harder to justify *Adderley*, in terms of advancing a legitimate governmental interest, than *O'Brien*.

If a peaceful demonstration somehow interfered with the building within which the legislature was functioning, perhaps by preventing the delivery of food which thus considerably slowed congressional peristalsis (surely the wrong state for passing wise legislation) then perhaps one might adopt the *Adderley* approach, although it may be useful to recognize that there are those who believe that only by inconveniencing Congressmen will one get wiser legislation. In any event, without having to pass upon a demonstration which does not interfere with the legislative process, there was no showing in *Adderley* that it interfered with the process of the facility in question and it was not a legislative process. It was, after all, only a prison.

IV General Theory for Legitimacy of Speech and Communication

In the constant and inevitable struggle between order and disorder, injustice and intolerable disorder are avoided by deliberately programming into the political system some manageable procedure for accommodating change. If change creates disorder and if it is still to be manageable while preserving important social goals, then the mechanism for change must be institutionalized and protected. In that way there will be less need to resort to dramatic and ultimate confrontations in order to achieve viability for goals which some regard as sufficiently important to jeopardize the stability of the system. It is in response to considerations such as these that the First Amendment freedoms are thought to deserve the privileged place in the hierarchy of constitutional values.

One of the primary characteristics of an open, liberal, mobile, democratic society is participation by the citizenry in the process of government. That entails, as a minimum, expression by the citizens themselves. Consequently, suppression of expression which is tolerated must be based upon a belief that a goal higher than those behind the First Amendment is served. The important goal of that amendment is the accommodation of change so that there will be only manageable disorder, hence suppression of expression must be justified by showing that the suppression serves this accommodation or some other equally important social goal. If access to the ideas market is denied, then even good ideas, which could have been implemented through the designated machinery, may be frustrated, and resort to violence is encouraged. If this analysis is reasonably accurate, then suppression of expression should require not less than a showing that violence is avoided by such suppression and that the suppression itself will not entail or escalate into even greater intolerable violence.

It is from considerations such as these that one may easily be led to regard as the most admirable alternative the position of Justice Black, who would give absolute protection to pure speech. Since by definition pure speech cannot include any violent conduct, suppression of such speech by appeal to the prevention of violence would be extraordinary. What I am suggesting is that when there is a question not of conduct but of pure speech only, there is no reason to suppress the speech. Even if it is necessary to proceed on an ad hoc basis for pure speech cases rather than to accord absolute protection, it is still difficult to imagine a case for suppressing a speech which did not amount to treason, because the social purposes of the suppression were more important than the purposes served by free speech. In addition, and as the minimum, when deciding between speech and repressive legislation, the least the Court should demand is what Professor Ratner has called "the least intrusive alternative." [68]

Hence, the view I advance is that there ought to be absolute protection for pure speech which is not treasonable and which is concerned with public issues, and that if such absolute protection is not accorded, then the minimum ought to be the least intrusive restrictive legislation possible. To this, I would only add that the speech must not be deliberately nor maliciously false. Therefore, pure speech (1) concerned with a public issue, (2) when not treasonable and (3) not deliberately nor maliciously false ought to be protected absolutely. There are two possible further criteria which may be relevant, but as they apply as well to communicative conduct, and since I am very uneasy about them, I will consider them last.

In this argument for absolute protection for pure speech, it is important to recognize that it does not imply there may be no regulation of pure speech. On the contrary, it is clear that there must be some area of legitimate regulation. The difference here is between prior restraint on the one hand, and suppression or regulation on the other. Absolute protection means only that there may be no prior restraint of content nor suppression because of what is said, not that regulation is also objectionable, nor even that suppression on grounds other than control are always unconstitutional.

As to regulation, it is necessary to observe that there are four distinguishable areas for possible regulation: content, time, place and circumstances. It is my opinion that short of treason, content should not be subject to regulation except to show that it is concerned with a public issue and is neither deliberately nor maliciously false. But as to time and place, speech may properly be subject to regulation. If a man wants to speak all alone and even without amplification at 5 p.m. on a weekday when traffic is at its height, at the intersection of the two busiest streets, I should suppose he should be suppressed; it is just the wrong time. At any time, it might also be the wrong place.

With regulation as to circumstances, it is necessary to de-

73

velop the difference between prior restraints, suppression and the post-restraint or suppression consequences of non-compliance. Let us call this latter aspect of the matter arrest-conviction. Since content is not subject to regulation, it is certainly not subject to prior restraint, whereas questions of time and place may be. If circumstance is to be subject to prior restraint the issue is whether the possibility of disorder makes permissible some restraint on speech. I believe that under properly drawn and sufficiently narrow statutes such restraint is legitimate. For example, A asks for a permit to speak at a given appropriate time and place. However, those responsible for the prevention of riot know that A's speech is likely to generate hostility in the audience and that without special preparation the situation could not be controlled. Requiring A to wait until the machinery for control can be made operative would probably be a reasonable prior restraint, provided the officials are not discriminating, they act promptly, etc.

Suppression is generally distinguished from prior restraint by virtue of the fact that the police or other officials must act quickly, without much, if any, chance to consult with legal or political counsel. When that suppressing official acts, he will generally do so under color of some generally pervasive criminal statute, rather than under a statute designed to cover speech or communicative conduct cases, per se, as when he suppresses to prevent or terminate a trespass or breach of the peace or to prevent illegal interference with traffic, etc. The relatively easy cases of suppression will turn on time and place factors; the hard cases will involve circumstances where there is an alleged danger of disorder.

Regarding the arrest-conviction aspect, the pure speech aspect of the situation will only seldom be a basis for arrest, as when there is a prohibition upon noise and the speech therefore violates the no noise condition, i.e., holding forth in the wrong place, e.g., a courtroom, or at the wrong time, 3 a.m. in a residential area. In general, however, the arrest-conviction aspect of a speech case will turn not on the sound component of the situation, but will depend on some spatial-temporal aspect of the speaker. For example, for the man who at 5 p.m. speaks at the busy intersection, it is the presence of his body which causes the traffic disruption. But as was the case for both prior restraints and suppression, the most difficult cases will concern arrest-conviction in connection with the circumstances where there is a possibility of, or an actual, disorder.

There remains now the question of when expressive conduct will be entitled to First Amendment protection. Here the issue is in part how to differentiate expression from conduct. Although one may not be convinced that Marshall McLuhan is right when he says that the medium is the message, one cannot but agree that there are important connections between the choice of medium and principles and problems of free speech.[69] As suggested earlier, lack of access to the media for reaching large audiences makes it almost inevitable that those who wish to protest social injustice as they feel it, may be required to engage in conduct of such notoriety that it attracts coverage by the mass media.[70] A Yippie recently suggested that even if there were funds available it would be wrong to purchase media space or time, since it is one of the principles of this kind of approach that space and time must be provided free by the media and the way to obtain media coverage is by doing sufficiently dramatic things so that the space is automatically accorded. In the trials involving those who counseled draft resistance, defense counsel for one of the defendants suggested that there was a privilege to engage in a particular course of conduct because it did express a view about social issues which was not deliberately nor maliciously false and not treasonable, even though it may have been extreme, because the extremity was the guarantee that the media would give coverage.[71]

There is another disturbing aspect to the question of distinguishing conduct from speech. Although we are certainly speech-oriented in the free communication of ideas which will enable the idea market place to operate effectively, is there not something essentially undemocratic in the view which favors verbal ability to communicate over all other abilities? If an individual lacks the ability to articulate his views in some sophisticated and intelligible verbal fashion, or in a fashion which will enable him to reach his audience, does it therefore follow that he does not deserve protection for the expression of his views? If a man is unable to speak at all but is an able artist, should his artistic expression receive only second-class protection under the First Amendment, whereas the skilled orator who is his fellow traveler is protected?

It would seem that much of what has been done to protest the war in Vietnam contributes woefully little to the debate on the issues. Many who participated in the anti-war demonstrations are inarticulate and often unaware of the issues, facts and background of the war in Vietnam. If the demonstrators were instead to have debated the real issues, very little would have been added to the intelligent resolution of the problem. But this does not mean that the protest demonstration which did not involve speech ought not be protected. It cannot be denied that such protests as marches, demonstrations, picketing and the like have focused attention on the issues and that such focusing has certainly had its impact in the shaping of public opinion.[72] Indeed it may even be argued that speech would focus attention on the issue much less successfully than mass demonstrations. Perhaps the question ought to be, Why should pure speech which communicates less effectively than does conduct receive the greater protection? Is the First Amendment to be read as saying that one may freely debate public issues so long as nothing effective is ever done?

For conduct which more or less effectively expresses views about a social issue, views not deliberately nor maliciously false, and where neither the conduct nor the communication is treasonable, should we then urge that such conduct receive the same absolute protection as pure speech? It seems to me the answer must be that expressive conduct ought also be so protected. Conversely, to the extent to which pure speech limitations may be warranted, then to the same extent may expressive conduct be limited and for the same kinds of reasons. For example, in *Gregory v. Chicago* when Gregory led a march to the residential area where Mayor Daley lived, the concurrence by Justice Black suggested that under proper legislation a state might prohibit "disruptive picketing or demonstrating in a residential neighborhood." If that be so, then I see no reason why pure speech could not also be prohibited there, unless "disruptive" modifies "demonstrating" as well as "picketing." But then, in that event, it would follow that if quiet, peaceful demonstrators precipitate a disruptive audience and may therefore be suppressed in an area which is "the last citadel of the tired, the weary and the sick," then could not a speaker be suppressed in the same place for the same reason? Yet the sentence immediately preceding the one in which the "last citadel" argument is made reads as follows: "Speech and press are, of course, to be free, so that public matters can be discussed with impunity." [73]

What I am suggesting is that for communicative conduct, the same range of considerations ought be relevant for prior restraint, suppression or arrest-conviction as are relevant for pure speech. In fact, almost never is the sound aspect of communication by unamplified speech the crucial factor in limiting absolutely free speech. It is rather the conduct aspect of a situation which invites or requires regulation. It is this which leads me to argue that the range and quality of factors which influence limitations ought be the same for public-issue speech or expressive conduct.

Consider the following cases: (1) A group of Yippies knowing that a meeting is going to be held to consider a particular problem "raid" the meeting and without injuring anyone seize the platform where they then "do their thing"; (2) Noting that a group of musicians will perform before a large audience in an area notorious for its suppression of certain fundamental freedoms (as conceived by D), D buys a ticket and at a propitious moment leaps to the stage, seizes the microphone and delivers an oration to his captive audience; (3) Wishing to express their dissatisfaction with some state of affairs, a boy and girl undress at the intersection of the two busiest streets in a large city; tattooed across their bodies are some words indicative of their feelings about the community; (4) At three o'clock in the morning, some very quiet demonstrators march in a residential area carrying signs which urge the mayor to fire the school superintendent. There is speech as well as conduct in each of these cases, and in each there is the potential for violence. How would these cases fare under the extreme theory of protection urged above which does not distinguish pure speech and expressive conduct?

What I have been arguing is that the criteria for the legitimation of communicative conduct should be the same as those for the legitimation of acts which are only speech, if the principle of the First Amendment is to encourage free exchange of ideas so that democracy can accommodate change by allowing persons to reach an audience in order to convince them of their ideas. What this means is that conduct ought to be protected when (1) the communicative function is reasonably likely to be understood by the intended audience,[74] (2) the conduct which is the vehicle for the expression is not itself a felony nor a misdemeanor which involves either violence towards a person or irreparable property damage, (3) the conduct is expressive of views about a public issue, (4) these views are not treasonable and (5) neither deliberately nor maliciously false. If there are any further limitations on expressive conduct, then the justification for such restrictions should be equally applicable to comparable pure speech. The two conditions one may add for expressive conduct which will be protected over those which obtain for pure speech indicate, I think, how one could definitionally deal with the requirement of absolute protection while at the same time minimizing inevitable ad hoc treatment of cases. The first condition, namely, that the conduct be reasonably likely to communicate a message to the intended audience, would discriminate against bizarre conduct unaccompanied by any speech element which might otherwise be thought entitled to protection. Thus, in the case involving the boy and girl who undressed at a street crossing, barring other offenses such as disrupting traffic, the conduct, excluding the language written on their bodies, would have been outside the domain of protected conduct, for merely stripping in a public place would hardly communicate any message other than that these two people were rather unusual. Whether or not having some message written on their bare bodies will save this form of expressive conduct from suppression is more interesting. If public nudity is not a crime, and if this boy and girl do not engage in conduct likely to cause loss of life or limb because of the hazards they create to traffic and since they are guilty of no irreparable injury to property, I think that even in this extreme case, the most that could be done to them is indictment for illegally interrupting the free flow of traffic or for creating a traffic hazard. Where the message communicated is not incidental to the conduct, and where the conduct is so clearly a violation of reasonable prescriptions, then the marginal communicative value ought not salvage the conduct. For this reason, it is necessary to add the second condition, namely, that the conduct be not itself a felony nor a misdeameanor of the kind which grows out of violence toward persons nor that which causes irreparable property damage. Thus, under the second criterion, assassinating a political figure, which has perhaps the highest communicative value, will not save the conduct from being a crime. Whereas a trespass to property without irreparable damage ought not itself defeat the possibility that the communicative component of the conduct does insulate it from prosecution for trespass.

Of the other three cases of communicative conduct, in the

first and second cases, while there may be some inconvenience, some disruption and certainly some impropriety in the conduct of the Yippees or Mr. D., with no felonious conduct nor misdemeanor conduct of the kind which creates irreparable damage or violence towards the person, it is probably better on balance not to suppress even the Yippees or Mr. D. We should not conclude from this that the non-Yippees on the podium in Case 1 or that members of the orchestra in Case 2 may not remove the Yippees or Mr. D. On the contrary, one is privileged to use reasonable force to retain the lawful possession of one's own property. And in both of these cases, I suspect, the intervention of the police to remove the Yippees or Mr. D. would have brought relief of the kind which was appropriate. What I am suggesting is that the subsequent prosecution of the Yippees or Mr. D. for anything more than trespass would seem to me to be a serious, unnecessary diminution in the rights of expression.

These cases, however, ought not to be compared with those in which the actor of the expressive conduct asks for protection. No one would expect the Yippees or Mr. D. to ask for police escort so that they could seize the stage in order to deliver their message. Consequently, what must be recognized is that when a demand is made for the protection of the conduct, then the power forces in the community should protect speech and expressive conduct as against encroachments or suppression when they satisfy the conditions I have mentioned. In the Yippee case or in that of Mr. D., protection of conduct entails that the prosecution be limited only to the specific violation of which the individual is guilty, and not be expanded because of the content of the message for which the offensive criminal conduct was a vehicle. There is a separate question about protecting expressive conduct in connection with repressive state legislation; why should the state create new crimes in order to repress expressive conduct? It should permit repression to occur only when the vehicle chosen is a violation of the prevailing laws as to felonies or misdemeanors of the kind mentioned in the criteria.

The most interesting problems may well involve trespass statutes, particularly those designed to protect public property. Without trying to deal in detail with specific cases,[75] much could be said for the view that where there is only a technical trespass to public property, and the purpose of the trespass is to communicate on a matter of public issue and the conduct is not itself treasonable nor communicating a deliberate or malicious falsehood, one could plausibly argue that the conduct ought not to be suppressed, unless the damage to the property by the trespass is irreparable. Since trespass seldom is irreparable, it would seem to me that this extension of the province for expression might well be indulged.

The difficulty here arises when the trespass is a continuing one, when, e.g., persons invade a draft board and continue to occupy it for a period of time beyond that of a transient trespass. This is a different case and one which should be dealt with separately. There can be no legal basis for protecting expressive conduct which uses the expressive conduct as the vehicle. The area of protected trespass ought then to be limited to the transient, technical trespass which is necessary or at least reasonable in order to make the message communicable to the audience to be reached. Continuing trespass, however, would not be within the same category unless no irreparable damage had resulted even from the continued trespass. One further matter which will affect conduct, but not speech, is that of disruption; i.e., since pure speech cannot disrupt legitimate governmental functions, but conduct may, when ought disruptions warrant suppression? The answer must be that suppression be permitted when the governmental function is sufficiently important to frustrate the objective behind the First Amendment, and when those engaged in the conduct could in no other reasonably effective way communicate their message. For reasons which I will come to later, I would also suggest the following further general principle: When the allegedly disruptive communicative conduct is concerned with voting rights or access to the franchise, then there shall be a presumption that the disrupted governmental conduct is not as important as the First Amendment objective.

Of the hypothetical cases mentioned above, the fourth is the most interesting. In a way it is related to *Brown v. Louisiana*, where there was a peaceful sit-in at the Audubon Library after the sheriff had been warned that demonstrators planned to stage this protest. Five to four, the convictions for breach of the peace were not sustained. The problem in the hypothetical case more than in *Brown v. Louisiana* is that although the demonstrators may be peaceful, they may be the catalytic agent for the precipitation of a situation in which an audience becomes hostile and noisy. So, at three in the morning, the demonstrators are perfectly quiet, having been conditioned, prepared, advised, and instructed beforehand, as Gregory advised his demonstrators when they marched on Mayor Daley's house, that they must be peaceful and quiet. So they utter not a sound, but their message is explosive and an audience gathers which is noisy. It is a case where the suppression of the noisy counter-demonstrators would be the preferable solution, but it may well be one which is unmanageable and therefore the question will be this: Can legislation be drafted, as Justice Black suggests, which would be sufficiently narrow to allow the police to suppress demonstrators who themselves are not in violation of any law because they demonstrate at a time or place or under circumstances which make the control of the audience impossible and where the audience may be engaged in the commission of conduct which is illegal, such as making noise in a residential area at three in the morning? As indicated above, it is my view that the demonstrators ought not to be suppressed but that the audience must be. Only where there is a danger of riot likely to result in loss of life or irreparable damage to property might legislation somehow seem acceptable which would permit the police to suppress the demonstrators after all efforts at suppressing the illegal counter-demonstrators have failed. This is very like the incitement to riot problem in connection with pure speech and further supports the view that if there is some further limitation on expressive conduct beyond those mentioned in the criteria, then the justification of such limitations would be equally applicable to the pure speech cases.

If the criteria for determining legitimacy of communicative conduct is not different from that for determining the legitimacy of pure speech, there will nonetheless remain a number of problems applicable to either speech or conduct, the legitimacy of which it will still be difficult to decide. Allow me merely to mention three such problems: corruption by obscenity, anonymity, and non-violent disruption by strategy. I will not try to offer any elaborate exegesis of the problems, let alone offer a solution. Consider the following cases: 1) Peaceful demonstrators carry signs quietly and orderly in an area which is not wholly inappropriate but which is contiguous to a grade school where the signs are highly visible from the windows of that school. The signs contain what many parents would regard as obscene language which they would prefer their children did not see. (Some of the signs also portray sexual acts.) Further, in order to dramatize their protest which is otherwise peaceful and orderly and probably protectable, the protestors perform sexually suggestive acts and deliberately display certain parts of their bodies to attract attention. Is the possibility of corrupting youth sufficiently serious to warrant suppression here when the displays and otherwise allegedly corrupting tactics are highly visible to children? In this regard, the *Tinker* case [76] is itself highly interesting. The young children involved in that case came from families where the parents were strongly committed to anti-Vietnam protestations, and it is worth speculating about the question of the scope of permissible parental influence and when that influence becomes corruption. At what point are the parents no longer free to commit their children to the political philosophy which may be incompatible with some long-term goals of the community? Or even when that is not the case, how far are parents privileged to use their children? Of course, this is the opposite side of the case I put, where no parents were engaged in the allegedly corrupting practice. What if, on the contrary, parents of the school children themselves were engaged in the allegedly corrupting obscene practices? Would this defeat the possibility for suppression of the otherwise peaceful, protectable demonstration? What if there were no obscene demonstrations but merely obscene language?

The next case is this: To what degree is anonymity antithetical to the interests of the First Amendment, so that where there is anonymity the otherwise protectable conduct would not be protected. A number of states do prohibit anonymity in political controversy. Under such legislation one may not march or otherwise demonstrate while in disguise nor distribute literature which is not signed or otherwise identified and still expect the protection of the First Amendment. There are some very interesting and very subtle issues here on when anonymity defeats the legitimate objectives of the theory of citizen participation via the market place of ideas. It does not require much imagination to discover that the quality of an idea is not necessarily connected with the identification of its author. Indeed, where the issue is not debatable and where the participation is not in shared ideas but in focusing attention so that those with power will react, anonymity is no more relevant than are dress or other incidental features of the demonstration. The theory for protecting such protests and demonstrations, such as peace marches and the like, is not that they contribute to the intellectual resolution of conflict but rather that they focus attention so that the power structure will respond to public opinion and thus retain its claim to legitimacy. After all, the basis for power, as I will try to argue later, is the support it finds in the opinion of the persons subjected to the power.

If this be the case, are not bodies marching enough to suggest that the power ought to respond or consider a situation? Why is identification relevant?

The last case has been called "the strategy of non-violent disruption." In both student protests and civil rights protests, many have been amazed at the lack of ingenuity displayed by those concerned with protesting alleged inequities. I will comment more on this in my second lecture, but for the moment concentrating on civil rights rather than student-protest phenomena, I think it worth observing that there are a number of non-violent maneuvers which could so totally disrupt many of the most critical functions of any organized political structure that it is difficult to understand why there has been no resort to them. Consider these tactics: Every day of the week, a request is made for a parade permit, a parade that may require a very substantial allocation of community resources to protect the paraders. A permit must be issued if it is to be a nonviolent peaceful parade at a right time and place, but the parade is clearly explosive because the protest is against an issue which is so controversial that the police and other public power instrumentalities must commit their resources to protection of the paraders. What if the forces in support of the particular alleged inequity must divide their resources if each day a different group requests the permission for a parade. Would there not be a serious diminution of community resources? Or suppose that all the persons who wish to protest a particular alleged inequity borrow the maximum number of books from the local library. They could virtually deplete the library in any library system and thus disrupt the function of the library. Or, what would happen if all the persons who wish to protest some alleged inequity flooded the police department switchboard so that "legitimate" emergency calls could not be handled? Or, if demands are made for police services which would so overwhelm the police department that it could not function, or the fire department, or other civil services which are to be provided by the city? What if all the legitimate health department complaints which are possible, were in fact made? What if every protestor took a long shower whenever there is a water shortage?

I raise these questions only to suggest that in terms of prior restraints, suppression and arrest-conviction consequences, it would be worth speculating on how matters such as these may be handled, and whether prior restraints or suppression would be permissible because of the considerations suggested by these cases.

I conclude by turning to the last aspect in any theory of criteria for the legitimation of direct action. You may recall that in each case where the speech or conduct was sustained by the Supreme Court, I mentioned specifically that the demonstration, protest or speech was peaceful. There is not a single decision which would support the view that a violent demonstration, protest or speech is protected under the First Amendment. As I have mentioned, from the beginning of the modern civil rights movement the Court has strongly supported the movement by refusing to convict for peaceful demonstration. But since 1964, the cases coming to the Court have increasingly involved issues of disorder, and the Court has consistently refused to review the decision of courts below where there was an element of disorder. The Court's increasing fear that the earlier decisions may have encouraged demonstrations which lead to disorder is strongly suggested by its sustaining the conviction of the demonstrators in *Adderley* and that of Martin Luther King in *Walker*. In these cases, there is the underlying, if not also sometimes even fairly explicit, recognition by the Court that demonstrations are likely to generate major disorders when the demonstrators confront persons whose views differ radically from their own.

No Court decision better illustrates the concern about the prevention of disorder than a most recent direct-action case, the so-called black armband decision in which the Court, speaking through Justice Fortas, sustained the right of school children to wear black arm bands in school in order to publicize their objection to the war in Vietnam. At least seven times in the course of his opinion,[77] Fortas returned to the theme that there was nothing in the record to show that this form of protest was likely to or did degenerate into or produce disorder. He said: "The wearing of arm bands in the circumstances of this case was entirely divorced from actually or potentially disruptive conduct by those participating in it." Later he added: "It does not concern aggressive disruptive action or even group demonstrations"; still later, "a silent passive expression of opinion unaccompanied by any disorder or disturbance on the part of petitioners." He further said: "the District Court concluded that the action of the school authorities was reasonable [in ordering the students to discontinue the wearing of the arm bands] because it was based upon the fear of a disturbance from the wearing of the arm bands. But, in our system, undifferentiated fear or apprehension of disturbance is not enough to overcome the right to freedom of expression." He added later that a student has a right to "express his opinions, even on controversial subjects like the conflict in Vietnam, if he does so without materially and substantially interfering with appropriate discipline in the operation of the school and without colliding with the rights of others." He also said, "[B]ut conduct, by the student in class or out of it, which for any reason—whether it stems from time, place, or type of behavior—materially disrupts class work or involves substantial disorder or invasion of the rights of others is, of course, not immunized by the constitutional guarantee of freedom of speech." In his concluding paragraph he remarked, "[T]he record does not demonstrate any facts which might reasonably have led school authorities to forecast substantial disruption of or material interference with school activities" and "[T]hey neither interrupted school activities nor sought to intrude in the school affairs or the lives of others."

If these statements do not adequately demonstrate that the absolute requirement for protection of communicative conduct is the absence of disorder, one need only read the well-publicized views of Justice Fortas in *Concerning Dissent and Civil Disobedience*.[78] Although not an opinion of the Court, this much criticized book probably expresses the view which the Court would now support. Conduct which is reasonably interpreted as peaceful and not likely to precipitate violence may well receive protection.

The position of the Court now is probably something like this: Where the communicative conduct is itself peaceful and not likely to cause disorder, it will be protected; but if that conduct is criminal, it will not be. If the defendant wishes only to communicate then there are equally effective modes of conduct which are not criminal. One does not have to loot a store in order to protest discriminatory treatment of people who are black. While it may be right to say that riots are "a communal expression of the ghetto's anguish" [79] it is unlikely that such a view will receive much protection from any court. The arm band, earlier sit-in and other demonstration cases where the Court refused to convict for trespass or breach of the peace are all premised upon the peacefulness of what was done. In no case is there a suggestion that violence is a legitimate device either to express or to focus attention, and that consequently, where these are a necessary part if not indeed the vehicle used for expression, they will not be legitimated by the Court.

You will recall that the general subject of these lectures is the legitimation of direct action as an instrument of social policy. In the 49th *Federalist* paper Madison argues that all political power rests upon opinion and that the strength of power is "in proportion to the number with which it is associated." Here is the clue to the determination of the legitimacy in these contexts, and why violence there can never be legitimated no matter what the claim is to moral justification.[80] The failure to distinguish between power and violence is what makes some think that there could be legitimated violence. But that cannot be. Power has its justification in the way it is used, and it may be wholly unjustified or even unjustifiable but it is legitimate or at least legitimatible. Power is legitimated action supported by past opinion. It derives its legitimacy from the conditions of its birth, not from the conditions of its use. Violence, on the other hand, is never legitimate but it may be justifiable. One must be cognizant of the distinction between justification and legitimation to understand why it is inevitable that violence can never be accommodated within a legal system which is a part of the power structure. There is no machinery for insulating violence by legitimacy, even when the power structure itself is not the object of the violence. Were the contrary the case, some criminal acts would not be criminal because benevolent. Because violence can never be legitimated the attempt to suppress violence by the utilization of power alone will not suffice and appeals to the justification for the violence will be irrelevant. It is therefore absolutely fundamental to recognize that violence will never be condoned by the power structure and that it will always be suppressed by the manipulation of whatever force the power structure has at its own disposal. When there is relatively equal access to violence then it may well be that the power will capitulate, but out of this confrontation no new power will rise. When that point comes, then the decision has to be made as to what could possibly constitute even the justification for what is in its nature inherently illegitimate, namely, violence.

In the United States today, it cannot be maintained that this decision need yet be made. And therefore to expect legitimation of violence is not only to expect the inconsistent but also something for which no power structure ever exists. Particularly, violence in the service of racism is an enormously destructive force. Whatever justification there may be for violence, it is almost inevitably short termed. The longer the term, the less likely there will be any significant justification; rather there will be only a reaction. In the service of racists violence tends to reinforce the racism, both because of the brotherhood created by the resort to violence and because the solution for the problems of racism is so long term that the appeal to those far-ranged justifications further entrenches the racist attitude. What makes the contemporary situation so explosive is the realization that the forms of social protest legitimated by the Supreme Court since the early 1960's (when the civil rights movement began), while an adequate substitute for violence in making *visible* the need for change, are not an adequate alternative to violence when it comes to effecting the legislative reforms necessary to alleviate the now visible and even acknowledged evils.

To expect the frustration which comes from being an acknowledged but powerless victim of injustice to find only peaceful expression by resort to legitimate direct action is to hope for the impossible. And if this were not enough to make recourse to violence predictable, there is the growing realization that de Tocqueville's law is readily applicable to the United States now. He said:

> Among the laws that rule human societies, there is one which seems to be more precise and clear than all others. If men are to remain civilized or to become so, the art of associating together must grow and improve in the same ratio in which the equality of conditions is increased.

Commenting on this Huntington says in his *Political Order in Changing Societies:*

> Social and economic change—urbanization, increases in literacy and education, industrialization, mass media expansion—extend political consciousness. These changes undermine institutions; they enormously complicate the problems of creating new bases of political association and new political institutions combining legitimacy and effectiveness. The rates of social mobilization and the expansion of political participation are high; the rates of political organization

and institutionalization are low. The result is political instability and disorder. The primary problem of politics is the lag in the development of political institutions behind social and economic change.[81]

The dilemma about legitimate direct action which affects social policy and the resort to violence is this: The kind of political instability which invites resort to violence is often the product of legitimate direct action which in making injustice visible, generates the demand for change, a change, however, not likely to result (at least in the area of race) without moving on to strategies beyond legitimate direct action. This illustrates the thesis that disorder is a consequence of the lag between political processes and social or economic change; the thesis here is that violence becomes an attractive alternative when modernization of the political machinery falls behind developments in the social and economic spheres.

Huntington, who develops and documents this thesis, quotes from Conroe who says of an unstable country that it is

One exposed to modernity; disrupted socially from the traditional patterns of life; confronted with pressures to change their ways, economically, socially and politically; bombarded with new and "better" ways of producing economic goods and services; and frustrated by the modernization process of change, generally, and the failure of their government to satisfy their ever-rising expectations, particularly.[82]

In the contemporary American situation, the non-white man's sense of frustration is heightened by the seeming governmental hypocrisy because technological innovations strongly support the belief that economic and social expectations can be fulfilled if only the government would utilize the technology at its disposal.

Urbanization, increases in literacy, education, and *media exposure* all give rise to enhanced aspirations and expectations which, if unsatisfied, galvanize individuals and groups into politics. In the absence of strong and adaptable political institutions, such increases in participation mean instability and violence.[83]

91

In short, Uncle Toms do not regard violence as a plausible alternative; but once legitimate direct action is brought live into his home by television Uncle Tom awakens from his a-political slumber; he is no longer Tom, let alone anybody's uncle. He is now armed with a new status; he is the generally acknowledged victim of injustice. What is more, this status has to some considerable extent been bestowed upon him by the Supreme Court when it did legitimate the direct action utilized in making visible the black man's claim to social and economic equality. Now, this same political instrumentality which helped create the new status is unable, by itself, to accord the satisfaction which that status demands. Even worse, the Court tells him that although he is constitutionally entitled to equality he may only resort to legitimate direct action to get what is rightfully his, and if he does resort to violence, then that same Court will sustain convictions for the violence used to attain that equality. As if this were not enough, there is the further exacerbating factor that the primary legal barrier to the realization of his right to social and economic equality is often the direct action by the states themselves.[84] This direct action includes refusal to take action and the failure to enact necessary legislation.

For politics and even religion (at least nowadays), it may suffice if legitimate direct action is the device available for making claims visible and for precipitating change. The contrary appears to be the case for racial equality. Whether there is this difference because race is more deeply embedded than politics or religion in our psychogenetic material, or because no process of political modernization is capable of accommodating a biracial society, I do not profess to know. But given the biracial reality without which our political processes must function, we have no choice but to try for the institutionalization of racial consensus rather than confrontation. Whether such consensus can accommodate some violence will depend in large part upon the extent to which black frustration, black rage, and even black racism can make consensus with the liberal mainstreams of American politics, so that white racism will not polarize around the issue of suppressing violence. I am optimistic about such a consensus because non-white Americans still overwhelmingly reject political fascism of the left or of the right and remain politically wedded to the main current of American political ideology. The kind of radicalism which these Americans have shown has not been so much ideological as political, in the sense of a commitment to militancy. But even here the militancy is directed not so much to new political systems as to achievement within the context of the prevailing value schemes. So my reason for optimism is that the dominant ideological and value commitments of white and non-white Americans are still sufficiently similar to make confrontation more objectionable than consensus.

The meaning of such consensus and its utility in making confrontation a less attractive alternative is very much dependent upon the degree to which non-whites are insured access to the most legitimate form of direct action, i.e., voting. It is for this reason I suggested that when direct action is aimed at the implementation of constitutional voting guarantees, the courts ought to tolerate the greatest possible degree of freedom, perhaps even refusing to sustain convictions for trespass or breach of peace which would be sustained were it not for the content of the particular speech or speech act. This is perhaps a dangerous suggestion, for I have urged also that content need not be relevant (except possibly where corruption of the young is involved). I now bring content back into the criteria for determining legitimacy, but with this distinction: I use content now to expand the area of legitimacy rather than to contract it as was the case during the hey-day of clear-and-present danger.

It is not my belief that the maximum possible expansion of voting rights for non-white Americans will insure the avoidance of confrontation.[85] Rather, my belief is that while such rights may not be a panacea, they may well be the most important single tactic in making consensus possible at the level where it is most likely to reduce the mounting tensions and frustrations, i.e., at the level of the smallest political voting unit. Control of communities is the cry, not control of the country.[86]

If non-whites may control their own communities and attract other like-minded persons to "their" community and repel persons of a contrary mind, (generally likely to be white) it may well be that de facto segregation will become the condition for avoiding intolerable disorder. However, between a constant and escalating state of disorder or economic equality with social ghettoization, there may not really be much choice.

III

Direct Action: Definition, Justifications and Explanations

by

Ernest van den Haag
Adjunct Professor of
Social Philosophy
New York University

I

To change policies, institutions, even the social order as a whole, groups may rely on procedures provided by custom and law or resort to direct action. I shall be concerned with direct action defined as overt pressure on the authority structure from below, by those subject to it or by affected outsiders. Pressures range from demonstrative symbolic acts and verbal dissent, or abstention from normal activities (strikes)—means usually regarded as not inherently illegitimate—to disruption and violence—means usually regarded as illegitimate.

The aim may be the enforcement of specific demands within the existing institutional structure, or modifications compatible with its general nature and function. However, deliberate obstruction of normal activities, and defiance of institutional rules (or laws) may be intended more generally to deny respect to existing authorities, to question their legitimacy or jurisdiction, and ultimately to abolish or take over their functions. To the extent to which that is the aim, specific demands serve as tactical instruments, reshaped and escalated whenever required by revolutionary strategy to mobilize support for confrontation. The role of Hitler's demands for rectification of the borders established by the Treaty of Versailles is pertinent here. The demands had merit. Yet to deal with them on their merits was to overlook that they served as means to position Germany for conquest, to divide the Allies, and to revolutionize the established European order. According to their leaders, the aim of some student groups today is revolution. The intrinsic merit of their demands does not matter then: they are used instrumentally as revolutionary tactics to achieve power.

II

In a nondemocratic political system, direct action may be the only way to produce political change. From a democratic viewpoint even insurrection—a comprehensive form of direct action—would be legitimate, because the system is not, since peaceful ways of changing it are illegal within it [1] and so are freely contested majority decisions.

In a democratic political system, direct action is antidemocratic (therefore illegitimate from a democratic viewpoint) if the change aimed for requires curtailment or abolition of democratic political processes, or ignores or overrides democratic political decisions. If the proposed change is supported by the majority, it does not require direct action, since democratic political processes would produce it.[2] If they do not, one must conclude that either the majority does not actually desire the change or the democratic procedures do not respond to the majority desire, i.e., are not actually democratic.[3] What kinds of direct action, then, can be legitimate in a democracy responsive to majority wishes?

Even if the political system is as democratic as can be, and all social institutions are subject to its laws, nonpolitical institutions such as families, churches, hospitals, schools, universities, labor unions or business firms remain self-regulating within broad limits. Within and among these institutions authority and power may be distributed in many ways and redistribution may be arranged through a great variety of procedures.[4] In the absence of other procedures, or to supplement them, direct action may be legitimate, both within and among institutions, to produce changes of policy and redistributions of power. Thus, direct actions limited in scope, with limited objectives, and by limited means, such as strikes (of workers engaged in production or students engaged in consumption), picketing, or boycotts, often have come to be accepted as legitimate and, also, as legal ways of bringing pressure to bear when better provisions for settling conflicts do not exist or work.

Direct action may be a legitimate means to change political institutions as well, even in a democracy. If a group is denied access to democratic procedure, and the remedies within the political system have been exhausted, resort to direct action need not be illegitimate. However, direct action as a last resort to obtain access to the democratic process must be sharply distinguished from actions aimed at defeating or replacing it, whether by groups excluded from it or by groups who have access to the democratic process but are displeased by the results.

Just as antidemocratic goals of direct actions are illegitimate in a democracy, so are antidemocratic means. Sit-ins, occupation of buildings, appropriation or destruction of property, invasion and disruption of offices, classrooms, or meetings, sequestration or expulsion of persons, and assaults cannot be legal or legitimate. Yet these direct actions are prosecuted only upon complaint of the aggrieved parties; and the persons and institutions concerned rarely are bold enough to invoke the law, or even institutional sanctions.[5]

Illegal direct actions have occurred in the past in labor-management struggles and in revolutions. Student riots have been with us since full-time students have. Nor are timid authorities new. But if the students are engaged in less than revolution now, they are also engaged in more than rioting (at least in something different). There are new elements which cannot be reduced to the familiar ones without loss of understanding. The occupation of university buildings or welfare offices differs from the occupation of the Bastille or the Winter Palace because it takes place without a revolutionary background; and it differs from the occupation of factories in the 1930's because it has nothing to do with workers, unions, employment, or wages. The contexts of direct action, the purposes, motives, and causes, above all, the identities of the activists are largely new.

III

The recent wave of direct actions (1965–1970) started in the South when Negroes used boycotts and sit-ins to claim rights still withheld there though long granted elsewhere. Their tactics were mostly nonviolent and nondestructive, and their law violations modest compared to those of their local opponents. Their demands—equal treatment, desegregation of public facilities, and access to democratic political processes—appeared justified, even overdue, to the courts and to most Americans.

Almost entirely excluded from democratic political processes, Southern Negroes were generally believed to have no alternative ways to press their demands. They were acclaimed in the North, where moral righteousness and heroism became associated with direct action. Soon almost any goal, to which egalitarian and leftist symbols could be attached, came to be regarded as justifying direct action. Direct action was used conspicuously to oppose the Vietnam war and became still more popular as the war became less so. Many pacifists and students who had participated in the Negro drive developed an insatiable appetite for protests against injustice and "the establishment"; they had found their mission and the means to pursue it.

Parts of the establishment began to back direct action. With the help of publicists involved in both the Negro and anti-war causes, President Johnson discovered there was poverty in America—in the nick of time, for poverty was about to disappear, unless redefined and subsidized more generously: one-fifth of all families were poor in 1962; in 1967 only one-ninth (5.3 million families out of 49.8 million) were. Mr. Johnson promptly initiated a "war against poverty." The major emphasis was not on helping the individual efforts of the poor to become less poor but on helping them as a group to claim subsidies and rights *qua* poor. The federal government, in effect, encouraged direct action to this end, at least against local government units, through its community action programs well described by Aaron Wildavsky:

> Have middle-class civil servants hire upper-class student radicals to use lower-class Negroes as a battering ram against the existing local political systems; then complain that people are going around disrupting things and chastise local politicians for not co-operating with those out to do them in. Get some poor people involved in local decision-making, only to discover that there is not enough at stake to be worth bothering about. Feel guilty about what has happened to black people; tell them you are surprised they have not revolted before; express shock and dismay when they follow your advice. Go in for a little force, just enough to anger, not enough to discourage. Feel guilty again; say you are surprised that worse has not happened. Alternate with a little suppression. Mix well, apply a match, and run. . . .[6]

Although most of the poor are not Negroes, most Negroes are poor; they tend to attribute their poverty to lack of opportunity (until recently with more justification than whites). Thus, direct action was spread easily to Northern ghettos, where it culminated in riots. White-run stores supplying the ghetto were looted and white owned houses in which Negroes lived were burned. According to President Johnson's investigating (Kerner) commission "white racism was essentially responsible." The riots were accepted—not only by the Kerner Commission but also by many government authorities, and by the mass media—as a deserved punishment for white crimes.[7]

Repentance and reparation rather than law enforcement were the remedies proposed.

The exoneration of the rioters, and the indictment of those rioted against should have encouraged further riots. If they did not occur to any great extent, the government authorities and the mass media were not to blame. The great majority of Negroes and of the poor do not read reports. Governmental and academic efforts to stir them up were only moderately successful because most poor people feel able to improve their situation by individual and legitimate efforts and therefore are not inclined to community action. The facts bear them out.[8]

Some of the poor do read government reports and many read the unqualified summaries in the press, while others are influenced by the incantations about the oppressiveness and the inequity of our social system, by which intellectuals express their dissatisfaction with their marginality. Many are prompted to direct action as they are convinced that "the system" run by "the establishment" cannot be changed otherwise.[9] The more literate groups influenced by these ideas gravitate around universities. Some are poor, some bored, some guilt ridden and marginal; all seek the gratifications of emotional commitment.

IV

It would be absurd to ascribe the seizures at universities to any single cause, or to hold all participating students and faculty members to be equally ignorant or irresponsible. More is involved than governmental promises, reports and academic versions of millenarianism. Direct action is a symptom of a great variety of problems, some chronic, some recent, some basic, some precipitating, some used as justifications, some unavowed.

Adolescents always have been most susceptible to what has

been called alienation (estrangement), anomie (rulelessness), acedia (apathy), or cachexia juvenilis (juvenile torpor) and, in more extreme cases, to dementia praecox (early madness, today called schizophrenia). To ward off withdrawal and depression, adolescents often hunger for involvement and activity in (instead of reflection on) reality, as well as for independence—a wish sometimes gratified by defying those already established.

By definition, adolescence is the process through which children exchange their familiar roles for unfamiliar adult, social roles. Even in a peasant community, where roles and transitions were structured by stable functions and tradition, where, further, the new roles were pre-established and well defined, transition was not easy. In fast-changing industrial, urbanized societies, where neither roles nor transitions are patterned by tradition, and where there is no stable community to continue any tradition, the task has become quite arduous.

Many adolescents do not manage to go beyond repudiating the parental roles, the established authorities and values. The de-cathexis (detachment) of familiar objects is easier and may not be followed by the more difficult re-cathexis of viable new ones. In some instances, neither is accomplished; and in the worst, the original cathexis was so unsatisfactory that no re-cathexis is possible—the classic setting of schizophrenia. In many cases fantasy-objects are cathected and the intrusions of reality—work, career, limits, obligations—are resented. A commitment to revolution is ideal in such cases: it produces a comprehensive sense of meaningful action, yet justifies the avoidance of everyday obligations and of discipline.

For students, the adolescent transition is particularly difficult. They must suddenly adapt to a whole new environment which challenges their confidence in received ideas, ideals, moralities, patterns of behavior, and self-conceptions. They are estranged from their homes, which are replaced by a temporary and unduly dependent relationship to alma mater, who seems demanding rather than giving, to the point of grading her children according to performance, and of rejecting those who fail. Students understandably grasp anything that permits autonomous self-identification and solidarity with newly significant others.

Fraternities and sororities used to offer communal support for the necessary transition from the family to individual, independent identification. They have been destroyed, often with the help of faculties who objected to the criteria of group formation (and therewith exclusion) and perhaps to the influence of the group on its members. The psychological need remains and group formation continues, even though less formalized. Are the criteria of inclusion presently used, the aims and activities pursued, the influences exercised by socially radical activist (instead of snobbish) ideologies and groups actually preferable to those replaced?

Poor (and black) students are likely to be least prepared for, and therefore most disoriented by, the college environment. Their initial self-confidence may also be lower; and they receive the least social support in the college. They may feel guilty about their families and friends; for these students can look forward to careers and comforts not open to their former associates, who are left behind in every sense.

Yet poor (and black) students are more interested than affluent ones in careers and future incomes and possibly in advancement for their own group. They have tried therefore to open college to more of their own, while seeking shelter from academic standards and obtaining privileges to enhance their status and self-conception.[10] A few of these students dimly realize that even when sheltered, they are unprepared to benefit from colleges with present standards. They are resentful enough to wish to destroy them. They are helped by not a few students able to benefit from college, who feel guilty about it, or bored, or, incapable of imposing the necessary discipline on themselves, or of accepting what they need.

V

Resentment is likely to become more frequent because more than 42 percent of college age youths now attend college—while only 25 percent of the age group have the I.Q. (over 110) required to benefit from college education. Many of these students, it is true, are still protected in community and junior colleges. But this is temporary. They will go on. Since education has taken the place formerly occupied by religion in the sentiments of many Americans, more and more money and people are pumped into it, without much thought given to the abilities of the participants and to the qualities and, above all, the actual effects of the education given. Education is felt to be good for everybody—by definition.[11]

Until college education is reduced to high school levels—and the process has only begun—more and more students will find college irrelevant to them. This will be unavoidable unless faculties realize that these students are irrelevant to the college. If they don't, college will become a custodial institution devoted to bull sessions and high school level instruction. The process is self-defeating, just as making national park lands overly accessible defeats their *raison d'être*. Americans have yet to learn that some good things do not remain good when shared too widely or with "irrelevant" persons, i.e., persons to whom they are irrelevant.

The college inflation was prompted by administrators who wanted to administer more and raise their prestige, by faculties who wanted to be promoted faster, as they will be, when there are more students (customers), as well as by our pan-educational ideology. Yet it is obvious to anyone familiar with the situation that far more people teach and do research than are competent to do either. Faculties and student bodies expand with available money and faster by far than available talent. The effect on knowledge may actually be negative: pseudo subjects are created, and pseudo scholarship creates obstacles to actual advances. The effect on students is no better.

College for everybody necessarily cancels the prestige and relative income advantages which rest on selectivity. Paradoxically, the disadvantages of not attending increase, as the advantages of attending decrease. The high school diploma today means little, but the lack of it means a lot. We find a parallel development with money; as people have more it means less. But not having it at all, being poor, is more painful than ever. So with the college degree. Wherefore we find some students attend college because they realize that a degree is required for anything they might want to do later. While attending they find out that the education certified by the degree is not relevant to their interests or future occupation. For four years they are kept dependent, and out of the activities they crave, to earn a degree required for, but not actually relevant to, their employment or to them. They are involuntary students, bored, and restless. Thus, the present college population includes, in unknown proportions (1) students who actually want (and benefit from) an education in the liberal arts; (2) students who attend for relevant vocational reasons; (3) students who attend for irrelevant vocational reasons—to get a degree required by employers (including the government) although what they learn (or, better, are taught) does not interest them and is of no actual use in their future activities.

These involuntary students are demoralized; they also demoralize others and are costly to education and to society. They probably could learn more outside college. They would not be compelled to attend if to the present prohibition of employment discrimination on the basis of race, a prohibition of discrimination on the basis of education were added: whenever education (or a degree) cannot be shown to be specifically relevant to the job, it cannot be used to discriminate among applicants. (The burden of proof would be on the employer.) [12]

VI

The students most dangerous to the university, at least in the short run, the students who resent it enough to actually attempt to destroy it through their direct action, are not those to whom it is rationally irrelevant but those to whom it is emotionally irrelevant—except as something to be defied. The psychological expectations of these students, inchoate and unconscious as they may be, are not met by the university and could not be met by any feasible institution of learning. They expect the university to save them—save them from tedium, from routine, from humdrum work and from discipline. They want the university to fulfill them, to direct them, to love them, to give meaning to their lives—but without imposing discipline. They expect the university to do for them what their parents did not—to listen to them. In short, they expect the university to function as an ideal, progressive kindergarten—and, bitterly disappointed as they must be, they are ready for revolution. With the exception of the blacks, the ideological and activist leaders of direct action are intelligent, affluent, and profoundly dissatisfied students emotionally disappointed by alma mater.

In the 19th century, Arthur Schopenhauer pointed to two major sources of human unhappiness: deprivation, which frustrates the poor, and surfeit, which causes the boredom of the rich. The poor are stimulated, or at least kept busy, but unsatisfied. The rich are materially satisfied but unstimulated. The poor wish for money and leisure to free them from deprivation; the rich for challenge and meaningful activity to free them from boredom.

In the past the rich were few, and many were still engaged in the activities which tradition and education, if not material need, had made meaningful to them. Now the poor are a minority—wherefore they are more resentful than ever. The newly affluent people keep busy, but find no satisfying ways to engage time, which hangs heavy on their hands. Unprepared for leisure they can no longer kill time altogether by making money—the challenge and the moral significance that gave meaning to this activity have diminished too much. Money has lost its authority (though not yet its power). Time stays alive to bore them. It bores their children even more: they never had to work out of necessity, and in many cases they have found no effort worth their while. The parents and schools who should have led them to meaningful efforts, to the discipline of work, to respect for achievement, have failed them. These children are desperate for the challenge of meaningful activity or, in its absence, for distraction from boredom, which makes time such a heavy burden to bear.

Sex and drugs serve to distract, as does the conspicuous consumption of the self engaged in by so many. But these do not yield the transcendent challenge and the sense of dedication ultimately required to ward off tedium, as Ortega y Gasset foresaw: "An 'unengaged' existence is a worse negation of life than death itself . . . before long there will be heard throughout the planet a formidable cry, like the howling of innumerable dogs to the stars, asking . . . to impose an occupation, a duty." We are surfeited with leisure, liberty, affluence and therewith boredom. The direct pursuit of pleasure turns out to be an onerous task for most of the young, and, in the end, is unrewarding.

Yet many students are unable to pursue anything else. Others fervently insist that everybody follow their ideals, which usually are generous and gentle, and so vaguely and gushily formulated as to be unobjectionable: peace, equality, freedom, creativity, love, sincerity, everybody doing his own "thing" (even nothing if he can't find anything to engage him). There is no understanding of the obstacles to the realization of such ideals, of their mutual inconsistency, of their clash with the requirements of any social order, of their unspecificity and ambiguity, which causes them to be beside the point and quite insufficient to solve the problems or devise the compromises which settle the conflicts of any feasible society. The only obstacles these students can see are the demons Marx secularized: oppressive capitalists, uptight racists and (via Herbert Marcuse) overly repressed middle classes. More love and more revolution will remedy all that.

Often students do not even wish to understand that to do nothing is to live at someone else's expense, off his labor; and that to demand as much as a right is to demand the right to exploit others. They meet objections with fantasies produced by journalism and science fiction: "scarcity" and, therewith, work could be abolished any day; or with the assertion of a right to be paid for a contribution not valued by others, of a right to be employed to produce something not demanded or to work at a job not available. It is not realized that this would exploit others by compelling them to give what they value—their work or its fruits—for something without value to them.

Similarly, students asserting the desirability of peace, love, etc., fail to see that no one denies it—that there is disagreement only on how to achieve and preserve peace, love, etc. It is simpler to picture opponents (the establishment) as hateful warmongers. Attempts to confront the actual intellectual issues are as rare as attempts to confront the dean are frequent. High ideals are used by flower-bearing, free, and thoughtless children to confront the parental generation involved in the sordid realities which made it possible for the children to concentrate on love and flowers.

At first blush one might conclude that instruction about the human experience with alternative organizations of society has been deficient. Ignorance, undispelled by education, certainly is part of the difficulty, and educators cannot escape blame.[13] However, the source of the problem is deeper.

Many students come from highly permissive homes which did not accustom them to value tradition, effort, discipline and authority. They learned to value intelligence, spontaneity, sincerity and freedom. But they were never taught to ask

> How but in custom and in ceremony
> Are innocence and beauty born? [14]

Indeed, they think of these as natural qualities. They learned, directly and indirectly, to

> . . . repudiate all versions of the doctrine of original sin, of there being insane and irrational springs of wickedness in most men. We were not aware that civilisation was a thin and precarious crust erected by the personality and the will of a very few, and only maintained by rules and conventions skilfully put across and guilefully preserved. We had no respect for traditional wisdom or the restraints of custom. We lacked reverence. . . .[15]

Lord Keynes became aware of the precariousness of civilization. Karl Marx did not, perhaps, because he lived in times less influenced by his own doctrines. (Hitler, and Marx's follower, Stalin, have shown Keynes right). Wickedness to Marx was not in man but in evil social, particularly economic, institutions and systems. Change them and beauty, honesty, liberty, love, peace, and equality will flourish, plenty will be produced, oppression, ignorance, greed and crime will vanish. The students follow Marx rather than Keynes, though with scant information and without his historical consciousness and intellectual rigor.

Often they veer toward anarchists such as Bakunin or Kropotkin. They all believe prelapsarian (pre-capitalist) human nature was good and postlapsarian (after the revolution) human nature will be. Many of these truly utopian students are naively religious in sentimental mood and moralistic style, while certainly chiliastic and antinomian in action. (Marx, by contrast, was pseudo-scientific in style, certainly a chiliast, but not an antinomian.)

The Rousseauean belief in paradise regained by freeing human nature has not faded; it has been recolored, e.g., by Norman O. Brown and Paul Goodman and various pop-singer poets (not to mention Herbert Marcuse). All of them appeal mainly to students. Stalin's and Hitler's versions of hell, and the purgatory of industrial mass society, have merely shifted the search of the true believers from economic to psychological grounds, while making them more impatient, irrational and humorless.

VII

The rejection of authority and discipline, which inspires so much utopian thinking, was generated by many sources, not least the permissiveness and the affluence in which so many of the militant students were brought up. The suburban middle class, most emphatically perhaps its Jewish component of *homines novi*, believed in science, and science was thought to newly support permissiveness and indulgence, to oppose frustration and restraint of children as well as discipline, punishment, and authority. The newly affluent parents also wanted to spare their children the hardships and restrictions they had suffered, the obstacles they had overcome, so that their children might remain idealistic. The parents succeeded and now their children have to create their own challenges.

Our rate of technological and social change is so high (and continuously accelerating) that the authority of tradition—authority is never less than a tradition—and of those bearing and transmitting it, was bound to be greatly impaired, and therewith, the authority of all established social institutions and values, particularly of the universities—the institutions charged with the transmission of knowledge, tradition, experience and learning and with preparing the young for established social roles. Our life has become too discontinuous—as has our culture—to grant authority to anything but present power.

When change is slow, the experience of the past seems applicable, and its bearers and transmitters are honored, its traditions revered. But a rapid pace of change makes the experience of the past seem obsolete. There is a loss of respect for those informed by it and a refusal to absorb what is regarded as irrelevant to "now." The old become old-fashioned, obsolete. So does the wisdom of the past. Why learn anything from the old generation, why learn anything old—isn't it altogether irrelevant to the now generation?

Actually, truth does not change, though our knowledge of it (what we believe) does. Some past beliefs are superseded; others are dropped as well, though no more than before known to be wrong. The attitude toward all ideas of the past, particularly the recent past, becomes negative. History is ignored. Thus we are condemned to repeat it by the young who push forward old discredited schemes that seem new to them. Typically, the ideas of a few generations back are touted as new. Grandfather's European get-up (as it appears to the young), his glasses, garments and beard are adopted. The young identify with his idealism and—where they do not seem restrictive—with his ideas. Parental affluence and business realism, parental experience and style, are repudiated in favor of the idealistic utopianism characteristic of the newly immigrated, who had no hope for improvement, except by changing the system. There is, of course, an oedipal air about this.

Meanwhile the social order is weakened by the increasingly radical questioning of the legitimacy of any standards of conduct, achievement and organization. The impairment of the authority of the past, of the traditions of civilizaton itself, is a basic cause of student unrest and ultimately of direct action the world over,[16] as well as an effect. Some students have become unable—never having been taught—to accept any authority. Many more feel that those now in positions of authority are not credible in their roles, that they do not actually possess the authority they claim. Students test them and often find their suspicions justified.

Authority is a relationship between those bearing it and those subjected to it, which disposes those subjected to authority to voluntarily comply with its orders and to support enforcement against those who do not. Such enforcement is regarded as morally legitimate when the authority is, and yet it is seldom required, since people are disposed to obey the decisions of an accepted authority.

Students now see university officials as shorn of authority, possessed only of power, which can be challenged and resisted: power bereft of authority invites challenge. When force has to be used against groups, the authority which wields it has lost, at least temporarily, its legitimacy in the eyes of the defiant groups. Timely and resolute use of force may restore authority, if followed by swift punishment of those who defied it, and by measures to reestablish its moral legitimacy. Whereas an early and credible announcement that resistance to authority will be broken by force can reestablish authority, concessions erode it. Negotiations under duress, any recognition of a right to direct action—even if implied merely by impunity—necessarily weakens authority further. Authority not enforced when resisted, or irresolutely enforced, becomes ineffective. It can be replaced only by naked power—which requires constant reassertion.

Originally just a few students tentatively defied university officials. However, these reacted irresolutely enough to discredit their authority in the eyes of all students, so that, when force was finally used, it too was defied. Concessions and amnesties followed and authority de-moralized itself altogether, even in the eyes of those who had not previously questioned it.

VIII

The original acceptance of parental authority occurs when the child still depends on his parents emotionally and materially. It is part of the learning process, of the socialization which takes place within the family. With adolescence parental authority decreases and is to some extent shifted outside the family. But authority cannot be shifted later unless it was established earlier.

When pushed too far, permissiveness, which encourages questioning more than the acceptance of authority, may cause the child, and later the adolescent, or adult, to be unable to accept authority altogether, however much he unconsciously craves it. Such persons become anxious, bored, rebellious and nihilistic. They directly or indirectly repudiate the parents who spoiled them, and defy all other authority, not just of persons, but of offices, traditions, procedures and customs. Finally, they force society to use the rod the parents spared.

In this sense, many students who rebelled against authority, unconsciously rebelled no less against its absence. Theirs was not so much a classical oedipal defiance, shifted to those who stand *in loco parentis,* as it was a defiance of the belated and incomplete imposition of social authority and discipline—when these notions and practices had not been part of their upbringing by their actual parents. Their rebellion was an attempt to organize their life, to find the missing limits, the discipline they were not helped to impose on themselves, the direction they were not given. Yet unprepared, they cannot accept what they need. Adolescents who never were taught to restrain their impulses, to take directions, may need and crave direction. But they resent the restrictions and directions that universities and societies must impose. They dream of a society without discipline or necessity, a society of pure self-indulgence ("love"), dedicated to sex, pleasure, and fantasy.[17]

IX

Actions occur only when the desire prompting them exceeds the desire to avoid the expected cost. The cost may be inherent (the effort to be made), economic (imposed by others to compensate for their effort), legal (penalties imposed by society to deter law violations), or moral (pangs of one's own conscience produced by violation of internalized rules). There are, then, two ways of preventing actions: by reducing the desire for them; or by raising the expected cost of fulfilling them.

The ability of universities to reduce the desire of the students for direct action is limited. They cannot control suburban education or social boredom; and many direct actions were prompted by matters beyond the control of universities, such as government policies. The students protested against university "cooperation" in such policies. Yet this cooperation usually was nothing more than academic freedom. Students and faculty members had the choice of working for or against government policies or of doing neither. The students opposed this choice: they denied the right of professors to make "immoral" choices, i.e., choices disapproved by militant students.

Universities as corporate bodies cannot struggle to change the social order or to oppose or endorse social policies—any more than the Post Office can. The campus cannot be (nor allow itself to be used as) an action agency, without ceasing to be a neutral research and educational institution, which permits each faculty member to select research subjects and pursue research (and publish results, or confide them to some, or to nobody); such research can be financed by the Civil Liberties Union, the Defense Department, or a labor union, as long as such financing is acceptable to the researcher. Similarly, the university must allow any career recruitment or none. It cannot make choices for its students or allow individual choices to be restricted by the wishes of majority or minority groups.

Not even a student directive to avoid investments in South Africa can be accepted. It is not among the university's tasks to exercise pressure on South Africa. The students are free to do so individually but not to impose their wish on the corporate body. If the student's moral criteria were to determine university investments, there might be few corporations the shares of which could be held; even government bonds might have to be avoided since some students oppose government policies. The money invested does not come from the students who wish to dispose of it. Nor does their enrollment entitle them to such disposal. Analogous arguments apply to the construction of buildings or other noninstructional university policies.

Students enroll to be instructed. Their only legitimate concern as students is the instruction they receive and whatever the university does to affect their life *qua* students. They are entitled to choose among universities though not to decide university policies—just as diners are entitled to choose among restaurants but not otherwise to determine their policies. Research is certainly within the domain of the faculty. Matters concerning the institution over a longer span must be the shared concern of faculty, administration and trustees, and only to a very small extent of any particular generation of students.[18]

Concerning instruction in American universities, I have never heard a respectable argument for letting students influence what is to be taught, or by whom, or who is to be admitted; wherefore I see no reason to discuss the matter at length.[19] If the patient (suffering from ignorance) had the competence he must attribute to the physicians to whom he entrusted himself, he would not need them. If he does not, he should not tell the physicians how he is to be cured or insist on the medicines that he prefers or regards as "relevant."

In European universities, students—whether competent or not—have a better case (though not necessarily a good one) because usually policies and curricula do not vary from university to university. Students have little choice.[20] But in the United States no student need subject himself to educational policies or curricula of which, for good or bad reasons, he disapproves. An immense variety of alternatives is available, and nearly every taste can be served. Student unrest here has more to do with the need of students to rebel against their own life and their society than with any curriculum.

Perhaps students should have been taught more about the functions of universities. But they do not necessarily learn what they are taught. Moreover, the understanding of many faculty members and administrations of their own academic freedom and of the obligations that go with it is less than perfect.[21] *Quis custodiat custodes?*

X

Since they could do so little to affect the desire of students to rebel, why did the universities not increase the cost of direct action? They could have suspended or expelled unruly students. Those who violated law could have been prosecuted. On the whole, universities preferred to allow their students to learn that the university authority and that of the law can be defied with impunity. Why?

The causes which led to the ineffective behavior of faculties and administrations overlap. The general decline of authority already has been mentioned. It is supported by egalitarian ideologies which confuse authority with "authoritarianism": illegitimate authority, or illegitimate use of authority, or the assertion of authority beyond its jurisdiction or in circumstances in which it is not needed, or, finally, the idea that authority must be total. The confusion between authority and authoritarianism was fostered, and, most important, authority was discredited by the emergence and the careers of Stalin, Hitler and Mussolini.[22]

Many officials also have a vague feeling not only that authority must rest on consent but that each specific act or authority must be ratified by a consensus. Rationally this would be absurd: the authority of laws and courts or universities rests on consent; but particular actions, procedures, laws, rules or enforcements need not. To think otherwise is to replace law and authority by consensus.

However irrational, the feeling that they could not act against what appeared as consensus was powerful enough among university officials to make them hesitate. It was reinforced by the craving for popularity dominant among mediocre people.[23] Such a feeling makes the assertion of authority against non-consenting groups psychologically hard, unless these groups first have been defined as being beyond the pale. Students clearly are not. On the contrary, administrators and some professors treat them as though they were a political constituency which must be catered to (to obtain reelection), or a group of consumers that must be induced to buy. The youth worship which has long been a part of our social life, borders on pedophelia. It makes it hard for any American to believe that in a conflict between generations the younger generation can be wrong; harder still to punish the young when more than a few deviant individuals seem involved.[24]

All these feelings were quite ably played on by the student activists. Because students seemed disaffected, faculties and administrations felt that they must have been guilty of some crime. The students hastened to define the crime as possession of authority and succeeded in demoralizing it. Professors and administrators searched their souls instead of asserting the authority of learning. Where did we go wrong? they asked; and each came up with a different answer. Most were eager to blame themselves, but for the wrong reasons.

In the "good" universities, where the activists are strongest, professors have been more critical of the authority of tradition —and of the tradition of authority—than their students. It was hard for them to oppose students who, somewhat indiscriminately, acted on their teaching. Some professors themselves are incapable of resisting actions to which leftist symbols are attached; others hate the administration and "the system" (and themselves) so much that they automatically identify with activist students.[25]

Academicians, moreover, are reluctant to use violence. The students, knowing this, used little violence (at least initially) but invited it by taking positions from which only violence could dislodge them. Many universities lacked the means, or felt they did, to deal with physically resisting students. Yet many professors also regarded the university as a sanctuary into which police should not be called.[26] They were willing to trust the students, regardless of their actions: my students, right or wrong. They insisted that rational discourse, not violence, was needed, although the students made rational discourse impossible. Obviously, direct action on campus owed as much to the weakness of faculties and administrations as to the strength of the students defying them.

XI

The reasons the students gave for their defiance confirm their irrationality.[27] They wanted community and individuality yet did not want to give up those advantages of an industrial civilization which rest on processes that are not, so far, reconciled with communal life. They were enraged by poverty, yet equally by technology and industrial production, which must be increased if poverty is to be reduced. They wanted community but also expanded enrollment; expanded enrollments but also smaller classes, and no physical expansion of the university. If threatened by the draft, they were enraged by the imposition; if exempted, they felt guilty enough to redouble their fervor. In short, the students were aggrieved by the human, the social, and the American predicament. But they preferred dreaming about chiliastic alternatives and engaging in senseless actions, to using the university for reflecting on feasible alternatives, none of which could have reached the perfection of the dream.

Let me turn to some of the arguments used. The *Cox Commission Report* about Columbia University quotes an anonymous student as saying: "Direct action . . . sit-ins and . . . physical violence . . . are political tools fairly comparable to the large political contribution, lobbying, favoritism, cocktail parties . . . used by the establishment."

It is true that cocktail party persuasion, used by the establishment, may achieve the same results as a confrontation used by its opponents. It does not follow that one "political tool" is as legitimate as the other. Rape may achieve the same result as seduction but does not therefore become legitimate. Persuasion (and seduction) at cocktail parties, or elsewhere, induces voluntary compliance of those influenced by it. Rape (or confrontation) compels (or attempts to compel) the victim to comply. One is force, the other influence. Rapists cannot justify (though they may explain) their action by pointing out that they are less favorably situated for seduction and less likely to persuade the girl (or the university) than a better endowed or richer suitor. Yet most of the argument for direct action is simply that persuasion might not succeed—as though this justified force.

Sometimes the idea takes a pseudo-sophisticated *tu quoque* form: [28] 'the present social order is maintained by violence or threats of violence; therefore those who use or threaten violence to destroy it are not guilty of anything that those who uphold it do not themselves do or approve'. Certainly both policemen and criminals use violence. But the latter do so to violate, whereas the policemen do so to defend, the law. To be sure, if the laws cannot be changed otherwise, the laws and the violence they legalize can be opposed, rightly or wrongly, only by violence. But if the laws can be changed when a majority wishes to change them, then violence takes the place reserved for persuasion and defeats the wishes of the majority. In a meeting in which every participant gets a chance to expound his views, the rules may be enforced by violence: those who hoot down speakers, throw rocks, or try to grab the microphone out of turn, may be physically restrained or expelled. But wherein does the violence required to defend freedom of speech (or any other liberty) justify violence used to attack it? A student's conviction of his own virtue does not justify his use of violence, even if he points out that he disagrees with the majority which, instead of doing what he thinks it should do, has the audacity to defend its right to decide peacefully—by violence, if necessary.

One final example, to show that Professor Marcuse is far from being alone in using such arguments. In a letter to *The New Republic*,[29] John Holt defends direct action by pointing out that the destruction of property by students is somehow not different from the destruction of "poor people's housing . . . by university expansion." A university's demolition of housing it owns (so as to construct buildings for expansion) becomes the same as the destruction of university property by people who do not own it. Yet Mr. Holt, although opposed to expansion of physical plants, favors university expansion: "Any educational institution . . . should be open to anyone who wants to make use of it. If . . . a student is not able to profit . . . let him make that judgment—just as I, and not the Boston Symphony Orchestra, judge whether I can make good use of . . . their music." What if the other students want to listen, but Mr. Holt wants to interrupt the (irrelevant) music, to insist that the program be changed? But let that go.

Certainly anyone who merely wishes to learn should be admitted to universities. This is done now for non-matriculated students in most places. If a degree (which orchestra listeners do not get) is wanted, obviously the institution must require students to have the capacity to earn it. It would be a waste of time to let students attend degree programs when they will not be able to earn the degree.

Suppose the demand for attendance at "good" universities exceeds their capacity. An orchestra in such a case would raise prices for seats so that demand becomes equal to supply. If the university is not to do this—and I am sure Mr. Holt does not want it to—what else can it do but select students by means of entrance criteria? Even expansion—about which Mr. Holt is so ambivalent—would not do away with the need for selection: if more students want to study with Professor X than he can teach, how can he be expanded? (The students, supported by Mr. Holt, already complain about large and impersonal lectures.) Adding students who cannot profit from study would aggravate all the present problems of universities and solve none.

The arguments offered by the student activists and their supporters are not better than those of Mr. Holt. There is little point analyzing them further. Their quality confirms what has been suggested throughout: the universities being the dwelling place of middle class adolescents have become the place in which these adolescents attempt to react to problems rooted elsewhere. Unfortunately the university authorities allowed their institutions to become the target of direct action, by failing to expell those engaged in it. But they are still in time to prevent the destruction of their institutions, and of the academic freedom that is their glory. The authority of learning has been impaired, but it need not be lost if its bearers free themselves from the curious superstition that physical force can be met by reasoning and that unreasonable demands and those who make them can be appeased.

Some students want to destroy the universities hoping thereby to contribute to the destruction of "the system." Universities would be remiss in their educational mission if they were not to teach their students that universities can defend themselves and that students are subject to law.

It is because of their virtues not because of their vices that the universities have become the first target of direct action.

Some of these virtues are connected with vulnerabilities (as are some vices): Free speech, teaching and research, independence from outside authority are both the glory and the weakness of universities.[30] Without these virtues they would cease to be the centers of research, reflection and critical intelligence which they are.

But people accustomed to the life of reason find it hard to understand that reason itself is not enough defense against unreasoning force, that freedom can be preserved only by the repression of those who seek to repress it by direct action. The universities hitherto have cultivated reason. Now they are called upon to defend their authority against direct action. Their success or failure will determine the future climate of our society: either we will be governed by persuasion and majority decisions which leave at least interstitial space for reason, or we will be run by the pressure groups that are able and willing to use the strongest physical means of disruption.

IV

Direct Action, Racial Protest, and Public Policy

by

CHARLES V. HAMILTON

Professor of Political Science
Roosevelt University *

* *At time of publication, Professor of Government, Columbia University.*

Within the context of the overall theme of this lecture series, I will discuss the function of direct action in regard to racial protest in this country. There are three major topics I wish to treat: direct action as a consequence of broadening the base of political participation; the crisis-reacting nature of our society; and the search for a new consensus and a new legitimacy.

I Broadening the Base of Political Participation

There has been considerable discussion—in the mass media, on college campuses, in conferences of various kinds—about the turn of the civil rights movement away from a legalistic approach to one of mass direct action. The discussion has emphasized the fact that there seems to be less inclination than before on the part of civil rights protestors to resort to the courts as initial instruments to bring about change. The observation is partially correct, but it is important to remember that the new movement has been essentially the result of the fact that newer groupings are involved in racial protest. It does not mean that those who traditionally pursued the lawsuit route have necessarily changed in their belief in the efficacy of the legal approach. One understands recent developments in racial protests more clearly if he recognizes that the considerable amount of direct action that has characterized the decade of the 1960's is very much a consequence of broadening the base of political participation.

As more and more groupings have become involved in civil rights protests, the groupings have served to fill a vacuum. That is to say, they have offered something which previous protest did not offer; namely, an opportunity for larger numbers of people to become personally involved. We saw this with the bus boycott beginning in 1955 in Montgomery, Alabama. Large numbers of black people not only stayed off the buses for over one year, but they attended weekly rallies, and they joined different political action committees (car pool, publicity, finance, etc.). This was direct action that served not to replace legal action, but to supplement it. In addition, invariably the mass direct action was predicated on *subsequent* legal action. This was, likewise, the case with the sit-in movement of the Southern black college students starting on February 1, 1960, followed in 1961 by the Freedom-Rides-in-the-South movement.

These direct action activities served as catalysts for subsequent politicizing work by newly developing leadership groups such as SNCC (Student Non-violent Coordinating Committee), a revitalized CORE (Congress of Racial Equality), the Mississippi Freedom Democratic Party and the Lowndes County Freedom Party. Increasingly larger numbers of people were called upon "to put their bodies on the line," "to come out tonight to discuss and make plans for a boycott and picketing of the downtown merchants," etc. And many came. In an earlier time, when legal action predominated, masses of people were not necessary for the struggle. A handful of lawyers, a few plaintiffs, and money fought "class actions" in the name of "all others similarly situated." And those similarly situated others remained relatively passive and uninvolved.

Entirely too much has been made of the proposition that direct action was a rejection of legal action. That is not correct.

Rather, direct action was a new mode of operation, a way to approach the problems of race in a manner calculated to activate more people. At all times, the direct actionists (in the late '50's and early '60's, as well as now) relied on the protection of subsequent legal action. The NAACP Legal Defense Fund and countless other civil rights lawyers were kept busy defending the prior direct action of the activists.

Many people can recall the years of the student sit-ins and Freedom Rides when part of the planning included lining up lawyers in advance to handle the myriad of predictable charges of trespass, disturbing the peace, inciting to riot, etc. Lawyers were no less important; they simply were no longer the sole initiators of protest.

One major aspect of political modernization is broadening the base of political participation. Societies that are modernizing are constantly involving more citizens in the decision-making processes. The civil rights movement in the 60's has been an illustration of this, and it was not only in the South that this was happening. Many sympathy picket lines were walked in the North in the early '60's against five and dime stores. And we began to see the pervasive spread of protest against Northern grievances in the summer of 1963, following the direct action protests in Birmingham, Alabama in the spring of 1963. People began to discover the "subtle" forms of discrimination and oppression embedded deeply in the North—in housing practices, employment policies, educational institutions, labor union operations, etc.

I put subtle in quotes because many black people never really believe that conditions in the North vis-a-vis black people were subtle. Simply because there were no signs on the wall saying "white" and "colored," then that made the oppression subtle; but that is only nonsense. It was real, live and right out front with black people who were trying to survive in the North. But that is the way it was described.

It was mass, direct action that served to communicate previously unarticulated grievances. Once the base of participation was broadened, it was clear that the sort of action masses would engage in, i.e., direct action, would begin to have a legitimacy not previously recognized. When the first four young, black freshmen at the black college in North Carolina sat down at a segregated lunch counter, to be followed by a few others, many people criticized them for defying the law, showing off, and admonished them for not taking their complaints to the courts. But more became involved, and the action took on a legitimacy in the eyes of many people in the country who had never bothered to think about the problems or who had at first thought the direct action was bad manners. And many can recall the numerous strategy sessions held into the night, discussing ways to make the direct action demonstrations more acceptable to masses in the country: should the black students dress neatly and carry their text-books with them as they sat-in? Should young children be used in mass marches in Birmingham in 1963? Should one go limp as he is being led off to the police wagon? Indeed, at one point, SNCC members adopted a policy of "jail, not bail" in order to dramatize further their sincerity and determination to the public.

The important point I want to make here is that more people, especially black people, were becoming politicized by these acts of direct action. It was not sufficient to tell them that they should resort to the courts first, or go to the conference table first, or rely on the ballot box first. All of those methods were being pursued in different places, but they were slow, protracted processes. And the results, even when favorable to the protesters, meant additional long years of implementation. Moreover, implementation was made much more difficult because the protesters would have to rely on a previously inactive populace. In more than a few cases, court battles were won breaking down the barrier of the white primary, for example, but there would remain a large, apathetic black populace that still believed "voting is white folks business." The direct action campaigns (marches, rallies, mock freedom elections, intensive voter-registration drives) tended to overcome this by involving masses and educating them at the outset; thus, when victory came (usually through the courts) the masses would be ready to move to implement those victories.

II Crisis-Reacting Nature of Society

There is a second aspect of direct action that deals with the perception of political reality of those engaging in the action. Many direct action, civil rights protesters believe that America is a crisis-reacting society. They believe that this country is prone to opt for the status quo in race relations or, at best, to opt for slow, incremental, token change unless confronted with a serious crisis which threatens order and stability. Thus, in 1946, a Virginia statute requiring racial segregation on buses within the state—whites and blacks could ride in the same bus, providing whites rode in the front seats and blacks in the rear— was declared by the United States Supreme Court to be an unconstitutional burden upon interstate commerce. (*Morgan v. Virginia,* 328 U.S. 373, 1946). But fifteen years later, black people were still being so segregated. Not until the mass, direct action of the Freedom Rides, with all the turmoil and violence —from local whites—leading to a series of crises, did the ICC finally issue an order on November 1, 1961 which led to substantial implementation of the no-segregation policy. We had simply missed the boat in our analysis of just what it takes to really stir and move society.

There was keen awareness, also, that the crisis surrounding the direct action protests in Birmingham in 1963 was the catalyst that led to the ultimate Civil Rights Act of 1964. It must be remembered that on February 28, 1963 President Kennedy sent a relatively mild message to Congress calling for extension of the Commission on Civil Rights and the tightening of loopholes in the previous laws relating to voting rights. But Birmingham (beginning in April 1963) and subsequent dramatic, direct-action, crisis laden events changed that. On June 13, 1963 Kennedy amended his proposals and asked the Congress to pass a much more comprehensive law covering voting and public accommodation. In July 1963, a provision dealing with fair employment practices was added. We know that these provisions have not been implemented fully, and this is so even for the voting rights provisions. In a number of counties and districts throughout the South, there are still many problems in getting the Justice Department to send in federal registrars.

It is clear that direct action protest has been met at times with violent responses from some white officials. These whites have done very much to create the crisis and thus to move others to action. Millions saw the water hoses and police dogs turned on civil rights demonstrators in Birmingham, and millions became indignant at Birmingham Commissioner of Public Safety, Eugene "Bull" Connor, who gave the orders. Dr. Martin Luther King, Jr. describes President Kennedy's assessment of the impact of this response. King wrote:

> This (civil rights) Revolution is genuine because it was born from the same womb that always gives birth to massive social upheavals— the womb of intolerable conditions and unendurable situations. In this time and circumstance, no leader or set of leaders could have acted as ringmasters, whipping a whole race out of purring contentment into leonine courage and action. If such credit is to be given to any single group, it might well go to segregationists, who, with their callous and cynical code, helped to arouse and ignite the righteous wrath of the Negro. In this connection, I am reminded of something President Kennedy said to me at the White House following the signing of the Birmingham agreement.
>
> "Our judgment of Bull Connor should not be too harsh," he commented. "After all, in his way, he has done a good deal for civil-rights legislation this year." (*Why We Can't Wait,* p. 144)

Unfortunately, but apparently true, it takes a crisis to begin to move the country toward an awareness that something *must* be done. It took the crisis of Birmingham for Kennedy to go on television in June of 1963 and to talk about the morality of the civil rights problems.

And even a crisis does not guarantee that effective, legitimate public policy will be forthcoming. In fact, the result might well be a kind of "backlash," wherein the white react negatively—after the fashion of arming themselves for a pending violent confrontation or going to the polls to vote for conservative candidates who vow to hold the line against progress in race relations, i.e., progress as defined by the civil rights activists.

If you really want to see the limitations of crisis, recall September 15, 1963. Many people know what happened on November 22, 1963: Kennedy was assassinated. But there are probably not 20 people present who can remember what happened on September 15, 1963. That was the day four little children dressed up and went to what is supposedly one of the safest institutions in this country, Sunday School. They were brought back with their heads severed from their bodies and their teeth knocked out. Many people in this country, simply said, "Tsk, tsk, tsk," and did not miss a step. Although few now recall the date of September 15, it was an incident which caused the commitment of many black people to the movement for black freedom, now. I am not surprised when a President or presidential contender, when Malcolm X or Martin Luther King get assassinated. Shocked and sad, yes, but not surprised; you expect people out front to be shot at. (The sociology people have something called the theory of role expectation.) But in a civilized society when you dress up your little ten-year-old girls and send them to church, you do not expect to have them brought back to you mutilated. And when that happens and society does not react in a morally indignant way, then all the fine buildings we can build, all the moons we can reach, all the fantastic gross national product and per capita income are

still worthless, because this is still an uncivilized barbaric society. When a society cannot pull itself together to react in a
positive, morally indignant way against an uncivilized act like
that, then the pledge of allegiance to the flag is only a travesty.

Very often the protesters are admonished to take their protest off the streets, i.e., away from direct action, and into the
conference room where "men of good will" can reason together.
Crisis, this argument goes, serve only to heat up the situation
and polarize forces. Professors Lewis Killian and Charles Grigg
in their book, *Racial Crisis in America,* give an excellent analysis of the relative impotence of biracial teams in trying to re-
solve racial problems through this method. Their studies of
racial conflict in several Southern cities in the 1960's led them
to conclude: "The biracial 'team' approach produces only a
superficial type of communication. The changes this approach
is likely to produce are insignificant in comparison with the
results of independent, aggressive action by militant Negro
leaders who approach the white power structure with threats,
not petitions. But even the new, 'protest' leaders with their
militant tactics, often win only token victories." (p. 105)

And their research led them to write:

> Paradoxically, this interaction within a conflict relationship seems
> to produce positive changes in the attitudes of the individuals in-
> volved. The phenomenon of developing respect for an able antag-
> onist who pursues his objectives with candor, courage, and integrity
> is not an uncommon one. White Americans may have to learn re-
> spect for Negro Americans as opponents before they can accept
> them as friends and equals. (p. 140)

One final point on this subject. I can recall many times
prior to 1963 when white people would say to me that they
could not understand the relatively nonviolent activity of black
Americans in pursuit of their goals. Those whites indicated
time and again that if *they* were subjected to the same kind
of oppression, *they* would rise up massively and violently.
There was a tinge of admiration for the blacks for their endur-

134

ance, but there was still a considerable amount of lack of respect—as I perceived it. With the development of mass, direct action, many whites probably do not *like* the consequences—crises, turmoil, violence—but many of them must *respect* the determination and commitment of the protesters. This is especially the case when one realizes the legitimacy of many of the complaints.

III   *The Search for a New Consensus and a New Legitimacy*

Unfortunately, in discussions of racial problems in the United States, not nearly enough attention is given to the phenomenon of political legitimacy. For the most part, social scientists have assumed the ultimate loyalty of black Americans to "the system," and the conclusion has been quickly drawn that what black Americans wanted generally was to get "in," to get a "piece of the action." I suspect this is very much true, if one approaches the matter strictly numerically. But it is very important that we begin to deal with the great possibility that significant numbers of black people, particularly the younger ones, who, of course, are more likely to engage in disruptive direct action, no longer see the existing political system as legitimate. I will cite Professor Seymour Martin Lipset's definition (in his book, *Political Man*) as relevant to my discussion:

> Legitimacy involves the capacity of the system to engender and maintain the belief that the existing political institutions are the most appropriate ones for the society. The extent to which contemporary democratic political systems are legitimate depends in large measure upon the ways in which the key issues which have historically divided the society have been resolved. . . . Groups regard a political system as legitimate or illegitimate according to the way in which its values fit with theirs. (p. 64)

Now, this definition is very important because many people

are saying progress is being made in race relations in this country and they point to all kinds of indices, Supreme Court decisions, speeches by public leaders, civil rights laws, and a few mixed marriages. But the important thing is not what decision makers say is happening. What is important is what masses of black people believe is happening.

Not only Lipset, but also V. O. Key in *Politics, Parties and Pressure Groups* (1942) as well as numerous other social science writers are making the same point. Yet, somehow or other, we just kept on defining the system as legitimate and imposing the definition on black people. Consequently, when on August 5, 1965, the Voting Rights Bill was passed and ten days later Watts blew up, many people scratched their heads and simply could not understand it: "We just passed the Voting Rights Bill." What these people did not comprehend was that the Voting Rights Bill vis-a-vis the lives of black people at 103rd and Central Avenue in South Los Angeles did not mean a thing. We might better understand Watts if we try to understand the perception of political reality of those blacks who are ready to blow up this society instead of being so smug about "American" values and the imposition of our criteria of progress on other people.

Now in this regard, we know where Stokely Carmichael and H. Rapp Brown are today ideologically. But we forget where Stokely was three years ago. He was in Lowndes County, Alabama and Greenwood, Mississippi doing what the people regard as some very systematically oriented things, like voter registration and freedom schools. How system-oriented can one be? I remember working with Stokely down there and having a contest to see who could file the most petitions to the Justice Department in any given week alleging voter denials and physical harassment of black people. The assumption was that if we filed those petitions often enough, voluminously enough, and accurately enough, the Civil Rights Division of the Justice Department would respond efficaciously. But it did not. It responded in its own way, slowly in some instances, rapidly in others. Stokely began to tune out. And so when people come up to me today and say, "You don't really believe what Stokely said, do you? All that business about the barrel of a gun—Do you really believe that? He's just a raving maniac, irresponsible, an agitated militant." I recall Lowndes County and Greenwood and our frustrations in playing the game according to the rules of a white racist society.

Increasingly larger numbers of black people are tuning out of the existing system. They do not see it as legitimate vis-a-vis *their* values and aspirations. Some data I have of beliefs of black college student activists are revealing. Among other questions, I have asked these activists (from 15 colleges, coast to coast, north and south) if they believed it important to vote for either a Republican or a Democratic presidential candidate. Of 251 replies, 52 respond yes; 199 say no. And in subsequent discussions, the latter indicate that they believe both major political parties ultimately operate to "hold the black man down," or "both parties are racist and cannot be looked to for relevant change," or some variant of these responses. Thus, to many of these activists who are prone to engage in direct action, electoral politics is viewed as a waste of time and energy.

There is today a crisis of legitimacy, a breakdown of consensus. Very many young black people simply do not feel constrained to play by the established rules of the game, because they see those rules as racist and the game as basically crooked and exploitative. When this becomes massively the case, those activists will feel less and less constrained in using direct action of the most disruptive sort. The system will respond by invoking the established rules of law, and from the system's point of view this invocation will be legitimate. But not to the activists, who are dealing with *their* notions of legitimacy and illegitimacy; the system is talking in terms of law and order. We must remind ourselves, however, that law qua law functions best in a *consensual* society, where at least if the participants do not agree with the content of the particular statute, at least they accept the legitimacy of the legislature to pass that statute, and of the executive to enforce it, and of the courts to adjudicate under it. Where there is no agreement on these fundamentals, then *law* will only be seen by the protesters as an instrument to be used for the benefit of the established power. This means, of course, that *political* governance has broken down, and what remains is only an ultimate resort to *military* governance on the part of the system. In such a situation, the protesters feel they must resort to "whatever means necessary" in their direct action campaigns.

My judgment, based on this analysis, is that in regard to direct action, racial protest and public policy, what decision-makers should be doing primarily is to try to work out a new consensual framework. Up to now, there has been a heavy emphasis on law and order. There has been a pervasive *un*willingness to accept the notion that very many of the existing institutions might be not only ineffective, but illegitimate. Time and again, *official* reports have documented the institutionally racist nature of many of the educational systems. Even the most systemically oriented political scientists have concluded that many levels of government decision-making have been oblivious of black people. There is a point beyond which we cannot continue to document the inequities of the society without expecting large numbers who have been the perennial victims of those inequities to become alienated.

Thus, I see very much of the direct action protest today as an effort to create a new consensus, as a search for new forms of legitimate decision-making. This consensus would overturn the entrenched racism of many of our values today. This consensus would accept as normative that every able-bodied and willing person is entitled to employment at a very decent income, and it would stop the nit-picking about whether government should be the employer of first or last resort. This consensus would include the normative value that not one human being in this country must go to bed hungry *any* night, or go without absolutely adequate medical care, or have to fight rats in tenements, or be denied an education to his fullest capacity. Until these normative values are accepted and actually implemented, this country will continue to experience a crisis of legitimacy.

In this connection consider what David Apter says in his book, *The Politics of Modernization,* where he talks about political legitimacy: When one is talking about what constitutes political legitimacy, one must deal normatively first, and structurally, second. This is a very important statement because we always ask the wrong question first. For example, we ask if one believes in the two-party system, a structurally oriented question, before asking about the normative values of the society. Or, to take another example, we have in this country a Head Start Program. It is a particular program and it has a particular structure. But notice how seldom we ask first the normative question, i.e., what are you giving those little black children a head start into? How often is there concern about the curricular content of those Head Start Programs? No, we *assume* the legitimacy of a white, Western-oriented culture, and we steadily try to make little, middle class, black sambos of those kids. When we do that, when we put the structure before the norm, we are acting illegitimately.

Finally, let me say this, the new forms of decision-making must come to terms with the fact that very much of the thrust today is not simply for an equitable distribution of goods and services. But if one listens carefully, the protests today are also calling for an equitable distribution of decision-making power. This means that many of the institutions today are perceived as illegitimate (recalling Lipset's definition) and they must be replaced with relevant intermediary groups. This could mean viable community control of schools, of law enforcement agencies, etc. It could mean actual community involvement in urban redevelopment. It really means that we must begin to

139

apply our talents to the fundamental task of viably restructuring our society. We must boldly ask the question: What new social units must or should perform what social functions—and to what normative ends?

All of this I see as the phenomenon of political modernization in this country at this time. I am excited (not frightened) by the process; I wish I could be sanguine about the prospects. Finally, since I see no acceptable alternative to optimism, I persist in the Lockian notion that man is basically rational, capable of knowing his self-interest, and capable, ultimately, of effecting a rapprochement based on that self-interest.

V

Direct Action on Campus

by

SAMUEL I. SHUMAN

*Professor of Law, Wayne State University
and Professor in the Department of Psychiatry,
in the School of Medicine*

I The Extent of the Movement

When I chose the topic for tonight's lecture, I thought it might be timely. And now, thousands of students across the country are laboring diligently to make my subject as timely as possible.

Contemporary student activism is one of the most interesting intellectual and sociological phenomena of the current decade. Whether it will also be important politically remains to be seen. Students have been active on prior occasions in other parts of the world, but American students remained apathetic (except about matters unrelated to political and social issues) until 1962. Whether the movement peaked out as Clark Kerr seems to think is open to debate.

In just over ten years, the university population went from about two and a half million to seven million; during the same period it doubled in Germany, England and France. At the present time, there is probably one new college a week opening which will mean about 500 colleges during the current decade. It is now conceivable that we will reach the goal of universal higher education. By 1970, when half of the U. S. population will be under 21, the problems of the only society in the world which has had to deal with mass-educated youth will become considerably exacerbated. There are now about 23 million

143

persons between the ages of 18 and 24, which by most standard definitions constitutes the so-called young generation. Of these 23 million, eight million go to college and of these eight million, about 60 percent, according to the *Fortune* survey, pursue fairly conventional career objectives.[1] The survey account is borne out by other comparable investigations, and the statistics are probably relatively reliable. The other three million plus seem to be differentiated from the more conventional students by their less intense motivation towards financial security and by their greater commitment to so-called social problems. Nonetheless, it is probably safe to estimate that nearly half of all college seniors are considering some kind of business career, which is probably not a significantly different percentage than obtained at prior times. The top academic people, from whom a large percentage of the activists come, were never much motivated toward business careers in any event and it is unlikely that the ranks of the business institutions will be seriously affected by declining recruitment possibilities among college seniors. For example, in 1968, over 25,000 seniors applied for 25 positions as account executive with Merrill Lynch, which seems to suggest that even for American capitalistic enterprise, there still seems to be no dearth of applicants.[2]

The number of students involved in activism varies. The *Fortune* survey suggests about 750,000 now identify with what is vaguely called the "movement."[3] Other investigations suggest that the number must be much less than that, somewhere in the range of 300,000 or 400,000. Either statistic is rather unreliable in that what constitutes the movement, as I shall suggest, is itself open to considerable debate, and what constitutes concern with the movement may be subject to considerable differences.[4] Seymour Lipset suggests that there are 30,000 students actively concerned with the New Left, with probably not more than 200 to 300 at each of the dominant university centers, such as Berkeley, Michigan, and Wisconsin, with less than 100 on most of the other large campuses.[5] The *Fortune* survey suggests that of the students who do make a commitment, not more than 5 percent would engage in conduct which might involve arrest. And not more than 20 percent would be active in any particular cause, although as many as half of the student population may be both empathetic and intellectually in agreement with the objectives of the movement. Clark Kerr suggests that probably no more than a third of the university students are actively involved in campus crises, and that in terms of faculty time or money the percentage is probably even lower than that.[6] If one concentrates on the clearly visible campus organizations, such as SDS, which has about 300 campus chapters, there are probably less than 7,000 dues-paying members or less than one-tenth of 1 percent of the American student population.[7] However, according to a *Times* story, SDS claims 70,000 members.[8] A Harris Poll of last spring suggested 2 percent of the students were activists. A Gallup Poll of June 1968, found that less than 20 percent had ever participated in any protest activity. Our survey here at Wayne State indicates that less than half the undergraduates have ever engaged in any kind of political or social protest activity.

II The Wayne Survey

The Wayne State survey grew out of the seminar in law and psychiatry which Dr. Eliot Luby of the Lafayette Clinic and I conducted jointly. Like myself, Dr. Luby is a professor in both the Law School and the Department of Psychiatry of the Wayne State Medical School. This year we thought it might be useful if we could expose our students to some experience in interviewing, since interviewing constitutes an integral part of a lawyer's existence. We originally planned a rather modest project, but because the subject became so interesting, we expanded it and surveyed the Law School, Monteith College (a special liberal arts college within the university) and the College of Liberal Arts. Our survey sample was limited to full-time undergraduates in Liberal Arts and Monteith and to the full-time day school population of the Law School. We selected a random sample by taking every 20th or 50th name from the roster of these colleges and sent a letter inviting the student to an interview which lasted approximately 30 to 40 minutes. This survey sought to discover the depth of university student commitment to political and social activism, the student reaction to some of the alleged activist activities on campus, their concern about the character of the university, and some specific questions about *The South End,* the student newspaper. *The South End,* at the time of the survey was an exceptional militant and radical college newspaper. The editor, while allegedly not a Black Panther, was a black militant, and the masthead of the newspaper showed a black panther in each corner. The content was often highly inflammatory; the newspaper was finally suspended by the president of the university.

Appendix I reproduces a not atypical item from the paper. Appendix II contains a summation of the statistical data on the Wayne survey. The full data, with cross-tabulations, is available.

III   The Movement and Who Is In It

Whether there is a movement and what its character is is less obvious than that its personnel is youth. As Kenniston points out, youth appears to be a new stage in life between adolescence and adulthood.[9] It is a luxury created by a technological and affluent society because a large number of adolescents who leave high school do not go into employment. Those who do are not "youths"; those who go to college or other pre-employment situations are the ones involved in the movement identified with campus activism. They are the youths coming into contact with the real world after the Russian missile crisis. They have the luxury for contemplation, the time and concern for politics and are thus unlike students in Cuba,[10] Israel, or Czechoslovakia, where there are no campus activists. American student activists seem to be concerned with problems which have always concerned society on prior occasions. But activist youths today seem to have a much greater intensity of commitment than their ancestors. Unlike their parents, the youths concerned with the movement have more freedom and are not required just to push out the old in order to accommodate the new. Nor are they different from the population as a whole. It is rather that they seem to be more anti-Vietnam than most people, more anti-bigness, more anti-uniformity, more anti-conformity, but not really different. The relative quiet in professional schools such as law, medicine and engineering is not difficult to understand in view of the fact that students there are less likely to be part of the youth population and resemble in many respects the people who leave high school for permanent employment careers. As Clark Kerr points out, ". . . the students who cause no trouble . . . [are] those of the working class or the lower middle class, the ones filled with tremendous vocational drive." [11]

Thus, those in the movement seem to be young people between 18 and 24, less vocationally concerned than those who enter employment after high school or those who intensively aim at the professional schools or are in the professional schools; they appear to be those young people in the undergraduate colleges, usually in the humanities faculties. It is of these youths that the question is asked, "Why are you so disorderly?" It is pretty much the same group of whom Justice Brennan says Plato addressed these inquiries some 2,000 years ago when he asked, "What is happening to our young people? They disrespect their elders, they disobey their parents. They ignore the laws. They riot in the streets inflamed with wild notions. Their morals are decaying. What is to become of them?" [12] Edmond Leach in his recent book, *A Runaway*

147

World,[13] suggests that the answer to this question is really quite simple. For the question is not "Why are the young so disorderly?" but "Why do the old imagine the young to be so disorderly?" Being close to the line, I should have been more sympathetic to his position had he not also added that "No one over 45 is really fit to teach anybody anything."

What is it about the movement which attracts the young? What do they mean by "the movement"?

Because of the number of groups involved, it is difficult to discover its ideals or even its membership. Some require dues, some are national and do not require dues, some are only local and require dues, some are highly organized, some are only loose coalitions, some are clearly political, some are apolitical.[14] It is in part this recognition of the diversity of views and commitments which has led one of the older leaders of the radical element in the New Left to argue (as Lasch does in his recent book, *The Agony of the American Left*) that a new political party is needed to bring together all the discontents who make up the New Left. The older radicals, like Lasch and Spock, still continue to believe that through the electoral process power can be gained. The New Democratic Coalition, with chapters in about 20 states, and the New Party operate in the hope that sufficient electoral power can be gained to effect objectives identified with the New Left.

Whatever else the New Left represents, a sensitivity about moral commitment is at its center.[15] The New Left and the movement among students regard morale as the clue to politics and generally see the destruction of political elites as an essential objective. They feel that power must be redistributed so that individuals have power over their own lives,[16] that blind power over each other is better than informed power by elites. A plank in the movement ideology therefore seems to be the democratization of power, which means at least direct participation in decision-making . . . a sort of New England town hall on a national basis. This sense of antagonism toward elitest power structures is not necessarily to be identified with economic or other leftist forms of radicalism. For example, Keniston found that conservative Republican fraternity types feel this same sense of alienation and even talk of emigrating to Canada or New Zealand to avoid a war imposed on them by leaders whose decisions appear not only morally monstrous but politically illegitimate.[17] The New Left appears to be more ethical or cultural rather than political, and for this reason it is essential to distinguish it from groups like the Maoists or Black Panthers. Despite its largely nonpolitical character, the movement seems to agree on Vietnam and civil liberties but only in the sense that there ought to be more civil liberties and less Vietnam. The New Left seems to be more optimistic about the quality of life despite the lack of any program for dealing with the generally pessimistic feeling about life in a large urban industrialized society. There is optimism in the commitment to be human, despite the crushing weight of large-scale, technological, political organizations. As some SDS students themselves have urged, they ought to be called the Jean Jacques Rousseau Society of Students for Small Society: they have no vision for large-scale economics. They are simply micro-economists, and the extent of their vision often appears to be a minibus of ten students who somehow pool resources and cross the country. Economics and political processes on a large scale are unattractive subjects and no commitment is made to issues of this dimension. This lack of concern with economics is not difficult to understand in light of the general lack of concern with improving the material welfare of the poor by utilizing science and technology, which seems to be a characteristic of many in the new rebellion. It is just this lack of concern about using science to improve material welfare which largely distinguishes this movement from prior revolutionary tendencies. Almost all such movements of the last 200 years were addicted to the theory that man's lot could be improved if only "science" could be applied to the problems of material welfare. The contemporary student movement and its adult equivalents reject science as a savior and indeed see in "big" science and technology a threat to the quality of life.

What I am trying to convey, is that these students are seeking a view on life and they want it now—no waiting.[18] They want to enter the classroom and in just 50 minutes be apprised of what the world is all about. They are unwilling to go through the sometimes painful, unrewarding process of building a *weltanschauung*. The idea of education is unattractive. They want their world delivered supermarket style: neatly wrapped and labelled—no grief, no frustration—instant *weltanschauung*.[19]

In thus portraying the youth of the New Left movement, I do not wish to be understood as saying that this somewhat Kafkaesque quality in their psychedelic world is without meaning or political significance. On the contrary, it seems to me that the New Left students have been a catalytic agent in society; they have been a significant force in the precipitation of a number of political programs. It may well be that Cohn-Bendit was absolutely right when he suggested why students have no political programs but act only as agents. In a famous interview with Jean Paul Sartre, he was asked, "Many people do not understand why you have not tried to draft a program and to structure your movement. They criticize you for destroying everything without knowing—or in any case, without saying —what you want in place of the institutions you have destroyed." Cohn-Bendit answered, "Naturally, the whole world would calm down . . . if they found that a party announced, 'these are the people who support us, these are our aims, and this is how we hope to achieve them . . .' then they would know what they were dealing with and could build a barrier against us. But the strength of our movement is precisely in this 'uncontrollable spontaneity.' "[20] While Cohn-Bendit probably speaks for those more programmed, more sophisticated, and politically mature youths involved in the movement, I have the feeling that most students are unaware of any *ultimate* program. Nonetheless, they share the feeling that out of the spontaneous rejection of bigness, belligerency, anonymity and elitist power, nothing worse can come than what we have, and therefore retaining the spontaneity which provides much of the romanticism of the movement is itself an objective to be courted.

In suggesting that there is a Kafka-like quality about the New Left and a psychedelic aspect to much of what is done in its name, I am not saying that activist students are psychotic. I am not convinced that Keniston is completely right in concluding that he does "not find much neurotic rebellion in the young people, but a principled radicalism." [21] I think he is more nearly correct than others who dismiss student activists as paranoid or neurotic, undisciplined, unmanageable, frustrated, anxious victims of irrevocable despair. What makes the activist seem anxious, and despairing or even neurotic, are the inconsistent qualities one detects in him; a commitment to an unspecified program for reform, a nebulous feeling that all is wrong but nothing can be right, a sense of unreality about his perception of other people and their conception of him and his objectives, and a sense of distance between him and the rest of the world, where the distance is not only political and social, but spatial as well. I dislike relying upon an overworked hypothesis, but in a word, for many of the activists, their seeming neuroticism is more like the despair of alienation.[22]

Unlike the alienated student of the 50's, the decade of silent students, the alienated student of the 60's sees activism as a source of salvation from his alienation and will become a dropout, an anarchist or a revolutionary—sometimes all three in varying mixtures. Upon entering college, larger and larger numbers of students, particularly those who have no intense vocational orientation, find an environment where they can publicly share their despair, apathy, meaninglessness—their constant unhappiness and boredom. They are already strangers in society and in their own families; their emotional life no longer connects them to their environment. Such students are likely to either slip or leap into one of several possible roles. They may become wholly alienated and in that sense mentally disturbed. This may be a role which suits quite a large number of students fairly well; this role is, after all, *some* role, and it does provide some attention. The sickness role is often the only device which such a student can utilize in order to make himself relate to some context which has meaning.

Where this role is rejected by the alienated student and where he does not become a drop-out from society, if not also from college, he is likely to be a marginal student with a marginal commitment to some aspects of the movement. He is likely to find anarchistic alternatives more attractive than revolutionary ones, and he may try to establish tight, but few, interpersonal relationships within which he can assert his identity and avoid the existential despair, which in more traditional, psychoanalytical language might be called the loss of ego identity. When there is a growing gap between what an individual really is and the idealized image he has of himself, the problem of identification and alienation is exacerbated, and the ability to develop adequate and rewarding interpersonal relationships deteriorates. Eric Fromm has often been concerned with the feeling of hopelessness which engulfs a man who becomes preoccupied with the realization that factors outside of himself make him the subject of forces which he cannot control, so that the feeling of being controlled on a string by the master puppeteer accentuates the normal realization that he is not God. Fromm emphasizes that we escape from these feelings of isolation and remoteness from the real world and attempt to control our own destiny by entering into relationships of reciprocal dependence.

Students who come to college from a family and high school environment which has already accentuated the alienating factors of bigness, jingoism, anonymity, boredom, meaninglessness and apathy, and who have survived the parental game of casting blame upon the "system" which has allowed all this to happen, are not likely to easily develop relationships at college which will suddenly permit escape from the alienating forces that produce feelings of isolation and despair. Such students are likely to develop some connection to the movement. Whether they will move in the direction of anarchy or revolution will depend as much upon the aspect of the movement with which they happen to come into contact as with their own needs. If the student's underlying personality structure is essentially inner rather than outer directed, he may find anarchism attractive because it distrusts and attacks authority and rejects the legitimacy of men ruling other men and particularly objects to elitist power structures (represented most vividly by professors and administrators in the university context). For such students, doing "your thing" by yourself becomes an end in itself, and the larger problems of social structure in a complex industrial society are unmanageable. Duberman in his history of American radicalism, notes this:

A final, more intangible affinity between anarchism and the entire New Left including the advocates of Black Power is in the area of personal style. Both hold up similar values for highest praise and emulation; simplicity, spontaneity, "naturalness," and "primitivism." Both reject modes of dress, music, personal relations, even of intoxication, which might be associated with the dominant middle-class culture. Both, finally, tend to link the basic virtues with "the people," and especially with the poor, the downtrodden, the alienated. It is this *Lumpenproletariat*—long kept outside the "system" and thus uncorrupted by its values—who are looked to as a repository of virtue, an example of a better way.[23]

The "Red Diaper Hypothesis" [24] lumps together activists from families in the 30's who were liberal and leftist, that is, "red." These activists are now celebrating in the streets actions and values only vaguely dreamed of by their parents—values largely associated with liberal, democratic virtues. After careful study of many activists, Keniston agrees that they often come

153

from liberal "left" families, although not from families which had a strong *commitment* to communism. In these liberal democratic families, the preferred value syndrome often includes a commitment to individual development, to spontaneity—a willingness to react to environment and a commitment to the realization of the self; there are few restraints on expression.[25] There is also a greater concern for the real problems and social conditions of other people. In such homes, children are encouraged to speak up, participate, and become committed. Whether such students will then become anarchists or revolutionaries depends on other family factors. Keniston suggests that if the student radical comes from a home where the parents are in the helping professions and the father is important, the student will become more radical. The alienated student is more likely to come from a home where the father is a businessman and the mother dominates the environment.[26] The mother-dominated student may either slip into outright anarchy or simply despair of political solutions altogether rather than commit himself to disciplined revolutionary action.

It is often the case that activist students come from liberal, democratic families, where the father is important and in one of the helping professions, and little, if any generation gap is found.[27] The attitudes, beliefs, positions and morality of the parents are often being acted out by their radical children. On fundamental issues, such as basic morality, the radical student is simply playing a role which the parents themselves favored at one time, if not now also. In contrast, the wide generation gap is more likely to be encountered if the student comes from a family which has facilitated his alienation and with whom he is no longer able to identify even on matters of basic morality, let alone on questions of politics. When this student enters college, he seeks out sources which reinforce his estrangement. Already alienated from his family, he may carry his alienation over to his surrogate family (the college) and then the question is: Will he become an alienation drop-out or move into the

one campus activist peer-group which will accommodate him—
the anarchistic element in the loose New Left movement.

One reason the New Left is so difficult to identify and deal
with is the emergence of a new generation of activists moving
into campus. They are coming not only from radical or liberal
families of upper middle-class professional people, but even
from more politically conventional families where there is a
more relaxed, more permissive life style and a decline in traditional parental authority structures. Such families often encourage a kind of soft romanticism to justify their lack of political and social commitment. Swept up into campus activism, it
is going to be increasingly difficult to identify the *meaning* of
the New Left or even activism, when these "romantics" become
involved.

It is worth noticing that when a *white* student activist makes
a commitment to some of the more revolutionary aspects of the
movement, his commitment is likely to be limited to revolutionary rhetoric rather than to conduct. Violence may be as
American as cherry pie but revolutionary violence among students certainly is not. Most of the middle-class students coming
from liberal or romantic families have never in their lives
punched someone in the nose, let alone fired a machine gun.
No student revolution has ever produced any final political
solution, with the possible exception of the Turkish student
revolts of 1955 and 1960. There are a number of reasons why
that is so. Modern revolutions, let alone student revolutions,
are almost never likely to be successful, because the moral, social and political issues which lead to revolution, as Goodman
points out in the last chapter of *Growing Up Absurd,* will almost inevitably require technical solutions to immediate problems, and thus the revolution will be unable to run its full
course. It is therefore much more fun to engage in the dialog
of revolution and to enjoy the romantic escapism of the revolutionary life-style without engaging in revolution at the level
which requires attention to the details of politics and eco-

155

nomics. Even Cohn-Bendit in the famous interview with Sartre pointed out that the revolutionary student did not expect to overthrow the bourgeois society at once, but to light a fuse and to show what could be done. The students did not even expect to control the revolution nor anticipate the connection with the workers as legitimate. Perhaps this explains in part why even the French communists first denounced the French student revolutionaries as mere "leftist adventurists." Only after the student revolutionaries showed that the uprising might have toppled the government, had there been professional revolutionary leadership, did the French communists identify with the clamor for public clemency for them.[28]

I have not developed the distinction between the revolutionary and the anarchistic[29] types within the campus New Left movement to suggest that there are only these two types. Indeed, the spectrum is considerably wider.[30] For example, Mr. Louie Patler, now a graduate student and instructor in sociology at Wayne State, after several years involvement with campus activism in California, differentiates some eight different types of activist. He ranges them from the nihilist who sees no hope of reform and who will commit murder or suicide (he thinks they are few but dangerous), to revolutionaries who though labelled "radical" are more likely to be only liberal, democratic and middle class. In addition, he distinguishes the innovative reformer, who will work within the system, from the defensive reformer, who will use civil disobedience to defend the rights students have gained. These are differentiated from both the manipulative reformer, who wants campus visibility as a step in his rise to personal success and also wants rights for students, and the student who is defensive about the status quo; his resort to violence is reactive rather than innovative. Finally, he distinguishes the alienated political like the Yippees, who are almost completely estranged from mainstream American life and protest via the outdoor theatre of the absurd, from the uncommitted alienated political who avoids political confrontation altogether.

My reason for laboring the distinctions among the campus participants in the New Left movement is that any rational attempt to deal with campus disruption or protest demonstrations cannot succeed on the assumption that there is a single explanation or even always a rational explanation for these upheavals. In our efforts to find criteria for the legitimation of direct action on campus, this must be born in mind.

IV   The Identity Crisis Within the Universities

Not only the activist students but the universities themselves are struggling through a crisis. The universities know they have lost their traditional function but do not know what the new function ought to be. They now resemble the medieval church: they must do everything for everyone. They are expected to become the all-knowing, all-enlightening, all-loving source for everybody. In modern times, cognizant of the fact that family, church, and government have declined in responsibility for leadership if not also in responsibility for moral direction, the universities have sought to fill the gap, or at least have had the demand made on them that they should do so.[31] They should become the pluralistic secular church (as Kenneth Arrowsmith argued in a recent lecture here). Mr. Arrowsmith would make this the function of the university and make those who create knowledge responsible for it. Rather than allow neutrality, passivity, and conformity to dominate the American university, as in the past, the university must become relevant. It must become the source of worldly wisdom, the source which in previous times was supplied if not by the family or by the church, at least by the government. With the failure of these institutions to "pollinate the mass," as Kierkegaard put it, something must provide the pollination, some bee must circulate among these flower children. What is left if family, church and government have failed? It can only be the university. The real problem in making the university the dumping ground for all the problems of society is this: What will become of the university? Can any single institution in our complex society perform *all* the functions which family, church and state are no longer capable of performing? Or wish to perform?

In a way, it is not surprising that the American university has been a target for all the disenfranchised, all the alienated, all the dissatisfied, all the disgruntled. Unlike the British university which concentrates on selected undergraduates, or the German university which concentrates on research and graduate training as the key to higher education, the American university has largely identified itself with service to the community, to some extent coupling this with graduate training in the hope that graduate training will contribute to the local community but also to the wider arena of American life. At least since 1876, when the university began concentrating on research and graduate instruction, it has had the double problem of teaching undergraduates and directing graduate research. However, even up to the Second World War, the university enterprise included significant commitment to undergraduate education; probably after that war, at least since 1945, there developed a sense of detachment, a sense of reserve about the university itself. Top professors no longer identified with the university but rather with their vocational specialty. They concentrated on developing what might be called the floating intelligentsia of university life where the commitment was to the field of specialization and its problems, rather than to the institution to which they were nominally attached. Organized research became the property of the professor. The professor was able to have a sense of mobility, economically and socially, as well as professionally, a sense which often came from getting funds for his research outside the university.[32] To the exaggerated importance given to such funded organized research and the decline in the emotional, philosophical and intellectual commitment to the university enterprise as a teaching institution, even when coupled with service, much of the problem in the loss of university identity can be traced. There are encouraging signs that younger faculty are more committed to their university; perhaps in part because they recognize that research in their special field is likely to be a young man's job, whereas tenure means they are liable to be at a university for a very long time. For example, in the hard sciences, a man will do his great research before he is 40 and still have 25 years left in terms of a commitment to a university. In view of the long-range possibility of association, perhaps it is encouraging to find that the younger faculty recognize the character of this long-range connection and are prepared to pour some of their resources into the development of the university as a place which will satisfy the emotional and intellectual objectives which their relationship was originally thought to encourage, i.e., the idea of the university as a place for education, not merely as a facility for research in one's private field or vocation.

The dean of faculties and provost of Columbia, Jacques Barzun, put it this way:

[M]aking the university more worldly has enormously increased the power of professionalism, both inside and outside the university. The Mandarin system is now in the saddle everywhere, and with all its usual features: vanity, self-seeking, faddishness, and the punishment for the naive, who are usually the geniuses. The contemporary spectacle of the curb market in prestige, with its bargains and bribes and daily ranking of man on the big board, is a reproach to intellect; and the goal of public service, which frequently leads to genteel prostitution in the halls of industry and charitable foundations, is no less a reproach to morality. We keep speaking of a company of scholars, but what we have in our new Babylons of higher learning is a scrimmage of self-seeking individuals and teams, the rugged age of guilded research.[33]

159

Perhaps Barzun overstates the case, but it would be difficult to deny that making the university more worldly and in some sense more democratic, has also contributed to the anti-intellectualism and greater activism of university personnel. The attempt to make the university a political adjunct to increasingly incompetent legislative bodies which lack the expertise available in the university and the increasing resort to the university as an instrument for the relief of all the problems which plague society have inevitably led to the destruction of the kind of university institution which at one time was thought to be above and apart from the demands of an active political environment. It therefore makes perfectly good sense for students who are activists to attack the university, because the university now stands as the representative of so much of vested political power. To expect that the university will be immune from the pressures of the political arena while at the same time serving as a contributor to the political arena is to expect more than is reasonable. When the university performed in its ivory tower context, it did deserve to be shielded from political pressures. But when it becomes part of the political process and purports to be a legitimate contributor to the solution of all the problems of mankind, when it stands willing to serve as a substitute for family, church, and government, then to expect immunity from attack because it was once a different institution, is to expect the impossible. What in some respects further exacerbates the paradox is that the university is not all just team research, politics, government consultation, big industry oriented, etc. Rather, it is a mix of all kinds of people, many of whom are still ivory-tower intellectuals who are shocked when their university is subjected to the political processes of activism. For them, the university never purported to be "relevant," as that term is now used, or more often misused, by some activists. For that faculty, still committed to the view of the university as a place for objective scholarship and excellence in teaching, the university was immune from political attack because it was supposed to be outside of politics. What is regrettable is that often the faculty most anxious to make the university what the activists call "relevant," are also the last to bear any of the burden when the university is attacked, because it is now an appropriate symbol of the relevant, but wrong, power structure. Those first to leave the university when it is attacked are often those who have access to other locations because their loyalty was to their field and not to their university.

If this faculty remained, it would probably make no difference anyway. For even those professors who do try to work within the crisis of confrontation, it is almost certain that after the initial involvement with the details of administration, their interest will soon evaporate when the excitement of the crisis evaporates; the continuing excitement of their own field will almost always prevail over the details of administration. Although a thousand members of the faculty may show up at Berkeley when there is a blow-up, the faculty senate will be back to the usual 100 as soon as the scene quiets down and the administration is once again making sure that the electricity is on and the hot water is running.[34] At that point, tracing the path of a new subatomic particle will generate more excitement in the professorial brain than operating the campus dormitory complex.

The identity crisis within the university had been developing for at least 15 years before the student activists entered the scene at Berkeley. Student disorders have only made the crisis more apparent and more urgent. Had student activism in response to Vietnam or other comparably provocative situations arisen 25 years ago or sometime before the Second World War, I find it unthinkable to believe that the faculty or the administration or the trustees would not have suppressed such activism without imagining that anything was wrong in doing so. But where the trustees, the administration and faculty share the apathy and indecisiveness, which comes from uncertainty as to what their job is supposed to be, what their position is in society and life, it is no surprise that they lack the authority, or, if you will, the legitimacy, to suppress demands which are either improper or improperly presented. The reaction has been one of embarrassment, not of authority or legitimacy. In the instances where the university has acted out of a sense of legitimacy because it has some conception of its mission, it seems to me the crises have been less severe. I think, for example, this helps explain why both Chicago and Pennsylvania were better able to survive the attacks on their integrity than have other institutions. It may also explain why the president of Notre Dame could, with relative ease, prevent disruption by simply issuing a statement which left little doubt that he had no reservation about the proper mission of his institution.[35]

Roughly speaking, there are four fairly typical styles of university administration. There are universities where the governors, regents, etc., determine fundamental policy; where a single individual, typically the president, does so; where the faculty exercise power over fundamental policy, and finally where the president and the faculty exercise the real power. Only occasionally is it likely that the faculty together with the regents, etc., will exercise such power. Where the administrative style is such that power is vested primarily in an apex figure or in a few, there is likely to be little or no shared consensus as to the mission of the institution and it will be difficult for the apex figure(s) to have any consensus out of which a sense of legitimacy can identify his power. Typically, in such a situation an attack on the dubious and insecure legitimacy of the apex structure will be met with extremist responses.

On the contrary, in an institution where there is some consensus as to the basic values which the institution ought to serve, even if the power structure is one which goes towards an apex rather than towards a broad power basis, it will be more difficult to impose demands incompatible with those basic values. In these situations it is less likely that there will be a need to call police. This in part, I believe, helps explain the relative success at both the Universities of Pennsylvania and Chicago when they were confronted by potentially disruptive student activism. For example, at the University of Pennsylvania, the trustees and the president were able to make significant concessions to the activists because they shared with their supporting faculty and student body a willingness to adjust and adopt in order to preserve basic shared values about the general mission of the institution.[36] On the other hand, where demands or even methods of presentation, go to the essential character of the institution (e.g., dropping admission requirements in favor of a contiguity test), then the probability of accommodations will diminish if not disappear, even where there is some sympathy for the demands among faculty and administrators.

The matter can perhaps be put like this: the greater the basis of consensus the easier it will be to accede to demands which do not attack fundamental values. The less the basis of consensus then, regardless of the demands, the less likely it is that there will be any accommodation. If the university neither represents a commitment to basic values, and only provides housing for professors who roam the field, and the university has identified itself as a community service facility and is failing in that, or if it acts as a substitute for a morally bankrupt government, it is difficult to imagine how any challenge to its precarious legitimacy can be accommodated. In such a situation, it is unrealistic to expect it not to appeal to the authorities, since there is so little authority in the university itself and so much in the police.[37]

I do not mean to suggest that if there is a sense of identity and institutional integrity, that the university will be spared. Were that the case, one could be more optimistic. The experience at Cornell, however, suggests that no such institutional integrity is an adequate insulation against deliberate confrontation and sabotage.

It is fashionable now for students to attack administrators when they are dissatisfied with situations on campus. I much prefer this to the alternative, which seems much more sensible, namely, to attack the faculty.[38] However, I have difficulty understanding the justification for the identification of administrators even as symbols. No one familiar with university administration or life in the university can have much doubt that faculty wishing to be active could easily dominate the administrative structure. By sheer number, if not by sheer intellectual and political power, the faculty could exercise decisive leadership in almost any area of university life. That they do not do so is explicable in terms of a number of different factors. First, it is more comfortable to have someone else take care of shoeing the donkey; second, it is more comfortable to be free of the complaint which comes from a donkey which has been shod carelessly. It is so much easier to complain about the electric service and plumbing than to be responsible for their repair. I much prefer having administrators willing to accept the responsibility for these tasks, freeing me for research, service to the community, or ivory-tower dreaming. That the faculty have so long been immune from responsibility for the institution with which they identify is difficult to understand except that for some reason college presidents and administrators are willing to stand on the firing line and accept responsibility for the shape of their institutions.

My difficulty in understanding why faculty have so long been immune from attack by student activists is heightened by the realization that for the kind of things the activists often want, administrators are much more likely to be accommodating and are more experimental and flexible than are the faculty. (Certainly this was true at Cornell.) The greater barriers to reform in higher education are the faculty, not the administrators; and so long as faculty are permitted to remain immune from responsibility for their institution and are permitted to fall back on administrators as a shield between themselves and reform demands, it will be impossible to reform university education. If social relevancy is the demand which allegedly underlines the moral basis of student activism, it is difficult to see why the activists aim at the administrators, who, compared to the faculty, are so much more oriented towards political and social relevance. These remarks are not intended as a defense of administrators but only to suggest that even if one is an activist it seems that much venom is wasted when aimed at the administration. In fact, I am not at all sure of what it means to make education politically and socially relevant, and thus would rather defend faculty who continue to believe in objective scholarship and teaching than relevant administrators. Convinced as I am that selective tolerance Marcuse style [39] is not better than selective intolerance Hitler style, I find relevance too insecure a foundation upon which to erect the scaffolding for university reform. Relevance strikes too many of the bells of history and all of them seem to toll the death of liberal virtues, including toleration.

Administrators do not insulate faculty from activists out of strong altruistic convictions about the need to shield their innocent faculties. Rather they do this, and the faculty allows them to do so, because each obtains from it quite exactly what each wants. In a way, the weakness of each contributes to the strength of the other. The faculty wants the easy deal which includes freedom from responsibility for the character and quality of the university, and the administrator wants freedom from the faculty in running the institution. Whether society should continue to ratify this bargain is perhaps one of the crucial issues which will come out of activist attacks upon the universities.

Administrators, if they wished, could make the faculty responsible for critical university policy and for identifying and implementing the mission of the institution. But rather than do that and take the anxiety-producing risk of the democratic process of decision making, most administrators (and faculty) prefer the consolidation of power which comes from having only token faculty involvement and which therefore permits the administrator to move the institution unencumbered by the need to consult any other power. The price paid for such a regime is that when confrontation comes, the lack of communication between the administrator and the faculty and the lack of inside support for him will almost inevitably compel him to stand in a position of isolation at the time when he most needs to operate from a context of consensus.

The disadvantages of this otherwise neat relationship emerge in crisis confrontations. Then the consequences of only token faculty involvement in central university policy making is glaringly apparent, that is, only token legitimacy for the administrator. A time of confrontation is hardly the best occasion to develop effective, durable and reliable channels of communication between administrator and faculty. Without such channels and some generally shared commitment to a conception of what the institution is for, the administrator's lack of authority inevitably serves to deteriorate the situation. To a considerable extent, what happened at Columbia is illustrative of this case.

V   The Legitimacy of Direct Action on Campus

Thus far, I have been concerned with the legitimacy of *power* within the university. Now turning to the legitimacy of *direct action* within the university, we can distinguish two different kinds of relevant criteria: those which relate to purpose and those which relate to method. Thus, direct action aimed at certain purposes might never be legitimate in the university environment. There are those who argue that if the purpose of a demonstration which disrupts important university functions is to protest American involvement in Vietnam, this would be improper because the connection between the university and Vietnam is so remote that the university ought not to be made the target for a disruptive demonstration. Of course, one could argue the validity of this principle on the theory that disrupting the university is disrupting the federal government because without the university and its experts the federal government could not function as well. But before discussing further the criteria as to purpose, I should note that there are surely some areas which are within the domain of legitimate direct action. The classic and usual first target of student reformers are the rules directed towards the regulation of the private lives of the students. It is entertaining if not also instructive to remember that the beginning of the revolt at Nanterre came out of a bedroom incident, i.e., the prohibition of the sexes to visit each other's rooms.[40] And while it is probably not the case that any university today is anything like Friedenberg's Milgrim High with its locked toilets and general custodial atmosphere,[41] there are probably still many institutions that fall short of the standard which ought to obtain, that "the student should be as free as possible from imposed limitations that have no direct relevance to his education." [42]

It might be academically interesting to look for other areas of clear legitimate student concern, like regulations on their private lives, but now that the university has identified with the community as a whole and the community's general value structure, the university is for students the most visible and therefore most appropriate target for protest on any aspect of life which they find objectionable. To think the university is protected because of its prior ivory-tower position is inconsistent with the new role which the university has either had cast upon it or willingly embraced. For the universities now to make a general disclaimer of responsibility for what they have become strikes me as no less absurd than the SDS position which would hold the university responsible for all the ills of society. As you might infer from the tone of these comments, I regret that the university has become the cathedral of modern life, for I should like to have the protection which comes from living in the ivory tower with all its alleged irrelevance.

If then, no purpose is outside the legitimate scope of some form of demonstration, the more critical problems will concern the legitimacy of methods in demonstrating. It is important to distinguish among dialog, disruptions and revolution on the one hand and participation, confrontation and decision-alteration on the other hand. The objective of rational student activism when it precipitates confrontation is either to acquire participation in decision-making or to affect decisions which have already been made or to make the university confront certain issues. Among the techniques used to precipitate the confrontation are dialog, disruption and revolution. Although there is not a hard and fast correlation among the alternatives and objectives it is probably the case that participation in decision-making is best achieved through dialog, decision-alternation through revolution, and issue confrontation by disruption.

Because dialog is so much an accepted part of university life, it may appear unnecessary to question its legitimacy. However, as I tried to explain in the second lecture of this series, the distinction between speech acts and acts which are connected with speech is sometimes very artificial. Since the meaning of legitimate dialog in campus confrontation politics has not yet been a serious issue compared to the other alternatives, it may be more useful to pass by the question of what legitimate dialog is and ask what, if anything, legitimate disruption or revolution is. It may appear inconsistent to speak of legitimate disruption or revolution, but as I tried to show in the second lecture, legitimate resistance to government is far from an inconsistency. However, in order to make sense of the seeming contradiction, it is necessary to have a functional meaning for legitimacy. In the context of campus confrontation, "legitimacy" means only that the conduct used to create the confrontation will not be the cause of any adverse consequence

168

deliberately imposed upon the actor, as an individual, because of his conduct. Thus, closing down a university as at Queens or leaving it severely debilitated as at San Francisco is an adverse consequence of the conduct which created the confrontation. But it does not mean that the conduct was illegitimate since the actors suffer this adversity not as individuals. Nor, in my mind should conduct be regarded as illegitimate in this context just because it could be the basis for a criminal prosecution. If the university has traditionally acted to protect from criminal prosecution panty raiders who create a disturbance, trespass or commit theft, then there ought to be no automatic conclusion that disturbing, trespassing or even stealing ought to make conduct illegitimate for a different but (at least) equally university-related purpose.

The conclusion then must be this: disruptive or revolutionary conduct is legitimate unless the conduct would be the basis for the imposition of a sanction by the university. Although this will appear to many as disarmingly simple, it is on the contrary a very powerful thesis. It implies both that the university may not rely upon the extra-university authorities to determine legitimacy and that it must take positive action in dealing with the issues. It is precisely these two points which are at stake in much of the most recent federal and state legislative concern about student activism. In New York, the legislature would apparently require the colleges to adopt the necessary rules on penalty of financial deprivations. Whether Congress will also do so is still uncertain.

These legislative maneuvers are not what interest me, but rather the fact that they highlight the unnecessary laxity by universities in failing to promulgate or even outline standards. The usual university student handbook is out-of-date and usually contains some omnibus clause about proper behavior. The 1968–69 *Handbook* at Wayne, "written by and for students" as the cover indicates, contains 146 pages. Of these, three are devoted to student rights and responsibilities; of these

169

three pages, 90 percent relates to grades and attendance. Except for four lines, nothing is very helpful in guiding a student who wants to protest. Those lines provide: "The University recognizes that the right of petition and the right to conduct a poll or referendum are vital to the free exchange of ideas. The University sets no regulation, either imposed or stated, which would in any way abridge these important rights." [43]

I am not suggesting that guidelines for protest would have prevented the turmoil at Columbia, San Francisco State or Cornell. I believe, however, that such guidelines make it easier to deal fairly with protest conduct and may deter some from participating in conduct which is clearly identified in advance as illegitimate.[44] One reason for the relative "success" of the six-day sit-in at the University of Pennsylvania was the availability of a student-faculty report which had been prepared the year before the sit-in occurred.[45] The report specified that activities which create a substantial threat of harm to persons or property would not be condoned and individuals threatening or causing such harm would be punished; that libraries, offices, etc., were not to be used for demonstrations; and that although the noise level of a demonstration was itself not a sufficient ground for suppression, it might be a consideration in affecting modification or termination of the demonstration. Further, because of the risk of damage to property, demonstrations should not be held in sensitive areas like laboratories and museums, nor where they would interfere with hospitals, communications or utility facilities, nor where there would be an acute danger from fire or falling objects.

The importance of readily available rules for governing protest demonstrations and for the procedures pursuant to which university sanctions are imposed is also suggested by the recent decision in *Barker v. Hardway*, where students were suspended as a result of participating in aggressive direct action. There, the Supreme Court denied certiorari and in doing so Justice Fortas specifically stated that "an adequate hearing was afforded [the students] on the issue of suspension." [46] The district court judge made a finding of fact that there was a student handbook which "set forth the rights of students to assemble, discuss, debate and to disseminate personal and group opinions; the right to initiate and conduct organizations . . . and the right to use college facilities in accordance with college regulations. Also included is a code of conduct." [47] I refer to this case here only to stress the importance of having rules available in advance. It is also of interest for other reasons, specifically, for its clear support of university-imposed sanctions for conduct which Justice Fortas labelled "aggressive and violent."

Once it is admitted that some forms of protest are legitimate as are some forms of demonstration, then the critical task for the university is neither to suppress demonstrations nor protests nor to convince those who demonstrate that they are wrong. Rather, the task is to provide principles which differentiate between legitimate and illegitimate conduct. One important reason why many colleges have not developed such principles is because the criteria for legitimacy, no matter what they are in detail, will presuppose a shared conception of what those functions of the university are which no demonstration may disrupt. As I have suggested, many universities today would have considerable difficulty identifying those functions and, therefore, probably rightly avoid developing principles which would only heighten the existing controversies. One possible benefit of contemporary campus extremism is that it may help crystallize faculty support for a renewed commitment to the tradition of objective scholarship and teaching. Indeed, a common reaction to the most recent wave of campus activism seems to be just such a feeling both within and without the universities.

Needless to say, there is no sharp line between disruption and revolution. There comes a point when disruption becomes revolution and it may occur an hair at a time or it may occur overnight. I have been amazed that students have generally failed to use any escalating technique of disruption but rather have moved from a relatively modest, harmless, disruptive tactic to extreme revolutionary action, like the seizure of a building. There are so many steps in between by which pressure can be increased without plunging into a revolutionary commitment which would compel confrontation on the worst possible terms.[48] Were I not anxious to avoid the charge of providing a manual for disrupters, I could easily spell out how to disrupt a university without immediately escalating from a mere sit-in to a revolutionary seizure. Just to mention one possibility, students could destroy a university if they all did their homework all the time: under such circumstances, most professors would want to leave immediately if they had to read all the papers students were asked to write and if each student turned in work of the quality and length of which he was capable. But even without going to that extreme of personal self-sacrifice for something as important as Vietnam or the right to smoke pot, there are many disruptive techniques between sit-in and seizure which could be very effective for compelling issue confrontation, participation in decision-making and even decision-alteration. One reason why students of the New Left so seldom demonstrate much imagination in connection with campus disruptions is because they seem to suffer from what may be called the Midas power complex. Power itself becomes an object of devotion and the desire for more power and more concentrated power becomes an obsession—rather than a concern with the use of power. Rather than using newly gained power to make some visible improvement in the university, the New Left seems obsessed only with gaining real power. The idea seems to be that reforms are not worth bothering with and that therefore only total change is worth the effort, and that requires total power. In this respect, campus activists so often seem to be playing the game of "If only I were king for a day—what would I do?" Of course, serious reform, which may require meticulous, detailed, long-range planning is much less fun than hit-and-run politics.

Implementation of my proposal for laying down in advance guidelines for the regulation of demonstrations may well be useless in preventing the precipitation of a revolutionary situation as distinguished from a disruption situation. When either the guidelines are frustrated deliberately or the guidelines are inapplicable because of a deliberate effort to propel the situation from disruption into revolution, then the interesting question will be "Is there any such thing as legitimate revolutionary direct action on campus?" In the second lecture I suggested that it was inconsistent to expect violence to be legitimated within the context of any authority structure because the notion of power is antithetical to the notion of legitimate violence. But this is not quite the same as asking whether revolution can ever be legitimated within the special domain of the university environment. If revolution means a commitment to violence, violence not in the sense of force, but in the classical sense, then the answer again will be no; there can be no legitimation for violence on campus. If the New Left or any other activist group is sufficiently committed to an ideal, or is sufficiently indifferent to all ideals, to be willing to risk the consequences of a revolutionary involvement, then "legitimacy" is meaningless; we would no longer be talking about the same issues.

In general, most student activists within the movement and SDS are not anxious for revolutionary confrontation, out of which the only possibility would be the cessation of all university functions. On the other hand, within the student movement there are some revolutionary activists who do wish to destroy the universities, either because they are nihilists or because they are true revolutionaries who want to close down the institutions, for to them no confrontation will produce the reforms thought necessary. The problem is further complicated by the weird admixture of student groups involved in a confrontation. If the university could be sure that it is dealing with a dominantly revolutionary group for whom the object of the confrontation is not decision participation, issue confrontation, or even decision alteration, but destruction of the institution, then it would not be difficult to deal with the situation. Then the regular university administrators or faculty should not try to deal with the demonstration but turn the matter over to the courts or even to the regents or governors. These are the force-manipulating instrumentalities; let them do their job. The university has no access to the kind of force which will enable it to deal with revolutionary confrontation and when it does try to deal with it, the institution always loses. When it is convinced that the confrontation is revolutionary and not merely disruptive in order to attain a goal, the best first move is to close the campus and let the political instrumentalities handle the situation. I do not see this as a capitulation or surrender at all. The university is no more designed or equipped to handle such cases than are the institutions of the courts or regents designed or equipped to teach.

The confrontation crisis always degenerates when the university attempts to use a force over which it has no control, e.g., the police. Indeed, calling the police is probably now recognized as a classic mistake, since calling police while the campus is still open serves precisely the needs of the extremist. There was little doubt that the militants at San Francisco State were anxious to have the police enter the campus in order to capitalize on the blind hatred of students for cops, a hatred particularly intense after Chicago. As the two authors who surveyed that situation with the greatest detachment suggest, it was "obvious to them that the militants were doing this." [49] Let me quote at some length from the most exhaustive examination of the 1968 French revolution. Seale and McConville say this in *Red Flag/Black Flag*, where they are describing the Cohn-Bendit incident at Nanterre out of which the final explosion developed:

[R]umors are spread on the campus that Cohn-Bendit was going to be expelled because of the Missoffe incident. There was a curious ambiguity in the militants' attitude: They feared repression and yet courted it. They wanted to provoke the authorities, but not to the extent of being totally crushed. In their minds, the Cohn-Bendit affair became fused with the suspicion that police informers were active inside the university. The enragés' counterattack was in characteristic style—original, cheeky, effective. Cameras were turned on the police, the photographs blown up, pinned on placards, and jeeringly paraded up and down in the hall of the Sociology Building on the morning of January 26. There were hasty confabulations in the administration block. Political demonstrations were not allowed on the campus, but how was this ruling to be enforced, when the crowd of rebels, now some fifty strong, seemed to be growing larger and noisier every minute? An administrative officer hurried down to call the students to order. There was a scuffle. He and his assistants were pushed about. Dean Grappin was informed, reached for his telephone, and called for police help.

It was about eleven o'clock before half a dozen gardiens de la paix arrived on the scene. One look at the mob, and they decided this was too big for them to handle: They must call for reinforcements. An hour later four carloads of armed police drove up, and Grappin signed the paper authorizing them to enter the university precincts. Little did he know he was playing the enragés' game. Like guerillas leading an infantry column into an ambush, the enragés pelted the police with anything that came to hand and, running before them, drew them onto the campus. At that precise moment the doors of the lecture halls were thrown open to release a thousand students for their midday break. Before their astonished eyes their fears of repression took concrete form: The police, the hated flics, were no longer a rumor; they were a fact. Anger exploded like a fire bomb. "Death to the dean!" they shouted. "A bas les flics! Non a l'universite des flics! Nazis!" Armed with benches as battering rams, chair legs, stones, and bottles, the student mob drove into the police ranks, separating them, swamping them, chasing them here and there across the gravel and the thin grass by the swimming pool into the parking lots. Windows were shattered, cars bashed about, men wounded in both camps. Defeated, the police fled from the campus. The enragés had become a rabble army.

The technique had worked in embryo; the strategy of direct action, denoted by a militant minority, had been put to the test.

Provocation had drawn repression, which, in turn, had rallied mass support.[50]

The moral of the message is not very obscure. The universities ought not be in the police business and when police have to be called, let the courts do so.

But the problem is seldom so simple as dealing with a clear revolutionary confrontation. Therefore, the task of the university is to prevent the mobilization of student activists into a revolutionary commitment. A disruptive demonstration designed to achieve negotiable goals or goals which are capable of implementation, must therefore not be treated like a revolutionary confrontation, for this will only serve to polarize it. That is, the university must not create self-fulfilling prophesies: treat disruptive activists as revolutionaries and they will have few alternatives but to act as revolutionaries. It is for just this reason that I find the recent pronouncements by President Nixon and others in his administration naive. They have failed to see the wide spectrum of activist types who are a part of the movement and have also failed to see that there are some types of activists and some types of protest which not only can be, but should be, accommodated within the university.

Admittedly, Mr. Nixon, his Attorney General and others are reacting to severe provocation. Disruptive demonstration, let alone violence, extortion, intimidation, and destruction are not what non-students expect from students nor from any segment of a democratic society. It is always difficult to retain the kind of control necessary to deal with explosive crises, especially so when the revolutionary activist is able to manipulate legitimate activists, e.g., when the SDS uses a Black Studies demand as a vehicle to attract support for a confrontation in which Black Studies is largely irrelevant. But the exploitation of other activists by SDS or other revolutionary groups is only a part of the larger picture.

That larger picture, I think, is the need to recognize that

176

the universities are engaged in a struggle to decide whether they shall continue to be committed to objective scholarship, teaching and the pursuit of excellence, or whether they shall become democratic institutions. In putting the issue this way, I frankly admit that in important respects the universities are not democratic. We can hardly deny that a greater degree of democracy would enhance our commitment to scholarship and excellence. Effective student involvement in decision-making is not inconsistent with excellence in education, although I must confess that I have not yet seen any reform in higher education attributable to student activism which actually enhanced scholarship or excellence. But then, to expect such reforms from students is to expect what neither the faculty nor the administration has succeeded in doing.

Another and related aspect of the larger picture is whether the universities will continue to function as one of the main depositories of liberal values, or will capitulate to the demands for the democratization of all public institutions. It is in large part because universities are so much dedicated to the perpetuation of liberal values, especially toleration, that they have been ineffective in dealing with moral absolutists. It is this commitment to toleration which has enabled absolutists who resort to violence to be effective. The press and public have difficulty understanding why faculty are so tolerant of violence in support of left absolutists, when they would not be equally tolerant of violence in support of extremism to the right. The answer is, I think, that the universities have far too long tolerated extremism from the right which had no need to resort to violence in order to attain its goals.

In view of the university commitment to tolerance and rationality, it is easy to see why universities have acted in a way difficult for the public and press to appreciate. If the man in the street or even the Attorney General would naturally react to violence and extortion by using both, he finds it strange that the universities do not do likewise. Yet it is just this that makes the university different from the man in the street. If democratization of the values for which universities stand is successful, then they will react like the man in the street. As for myself, there are times when neither the man in the street nor the Attorney General is the highest or best authority.

Let me add a word on activism and violence. Violence is an umbrella under which many different degrees of disruption can stand. I have tried to suggest that violence itself is not the test of whether there is a revolutionary confrontation (the object of which is to close down the university). I have also suggested that without a revolutionary situation, the university ought to try and accommodate even a disruptive demonstration when its goals are at least theoretically capable of accommodation without abandoning the basic values of objective scholarship, teaching and excellence. This seems to me an attractive and plausible generalization with which to begin, even when the disruption entails some violence and so long as that violence does not create an imminent and uncontrollable danger to life or limb or irreparable or grossly unreasonable property damage. Although it is outrageous to accommodate demands made under extortion, it would be more outrageous for a university to compromise itself and what it stands for by responding to the method of making the demands rather than to the content of those demands. It is something like the controversy over the death penalty: the issue for those who do not favor it is not whether the criminal deserves to die but rather whether giving him what he deserves may require that we become what we do not deserve to be.

Those whose demands are made with violence and extortion may not deserve to have their demands met, but the university accommodates reasonable demands not for the demonstrators but for the university. For myself, I would not be very disturbed if the university were to expel dangerously violent students even while making the changes they sought. Being right is not an adequate excuse for being violent. Moral and

178

political absolutists may be right and what they demand should be done when they are right, but activists who think their absolutism serves as a defense for fascism, be it of the left or right, do not have a permanent place in American universities.[51] Whether they can be accommodated in some higher education process is an interesting but different question. Perhaps society ought to allocate some resource to see if they can be educated in an educational environment of the type they allegedly seek.

VI Suggestions Towards a Conclusion

There are a number of different types of student and community demands now being made upon the universities under the catchall label of campus activism. These demands are of two different kinds: institutional reforms and reforms of the institution. Now most frequently at the forefront are these:
   A. Institutional reforms:
      1. Abandonment of the loco parentis theory;
      2. Severance of the ties between the university and certain non-university agencies;
      3. Revitalization of undergraduate instruction.
   B. Reforms of the institution (democratization demands):
      4. Self-determination for students;
      5. Contiguity admission policies instead of admission standards;
      6. Special programs for the poor and non-white.
There are two additional kinds of demands which are either or both A and B:
      7. Black studies;
      8. Relevance and a commitment to a sense of morality.
   In terms of manageable campus disruption, had the universities responded to symptoms which were so clear and so appalling and of such long standing in the field of internal

reform (the first three demands), they may well have been spared some of the unmanageable disruptions. Because the heart of the contemporary disruptions is in the second three demands, I do not myself believe that these unmanageable disruptions would have been avoided, but their severity and frequency would certainly have been lessened. In part because the first three demands are often so reasonable and so readily accommodated within the general principles of the university, I regard them as distinguished from the demands for the democratization of the institution. Most universities today would like to dispense altogether with the burden of regulating their students' private lives. The one instance where regulation may continue to be a problem is where the university is located in a rural area and must provide a social as well as an intellectual environment for students, which forces it to act like a parent. This is an area which could readily be managed without precipitating any disruptive student activism. Particularly is this so if universities continue to make the students themselves responsible for the moral qualities of the social functions which the university sponsors.

The more critical problem in connection with institutional reforms concerns the severance of ties with outside agencies. I do not wish to be understood as supporting the extreme view that the university ought to have no defense, corporation, or foundation-funded research.[52] The criterion for accepting research projects ought to be whether the research serves the purposes and ideals of the university rather than some other aspect of the community, be it for defense, corporations or otherwise. The test should simply be whether the research advances the passionate commitment to the life of the mind and to the discipline of excellence, objective scholarship and teaching.[53] I see nothing special about research for war or research for peace or research for General Motors or research for the Institute for the Blind. The criterion ought to be the same in all cases. Will the research contribute to the university? Not vice versa. The importance of the research for the community as a whole does not mitigate for or against that research being done. It mitigates only against the research being done in the name and on the time of and with the resources of the university.

An especially vexing and difficult current problem concerning universities and research centers in what is sometimes called the "urban commitment." That is, universities located in urban areas have a special duty to devote their resources to the solution of the allegedly special problems of the cities; they must have departments on urban affairs which do research in that area. The difficulty here is this: there is not "the" university which should have an urban commitment. In varying degrees "the" university is no more than a collection of institutional departments using the same letterhead—and often even that is not true. To expect "the" university to do urban research ignores this reality and unnecessarily generates a feeling of alienation between some of the faculty and the university. Whether departmental independence is desirable or necessary even for a university is a large and largely ignored question. But the existence of such independence cannot be ignored when demands are made for a commitment from "the" university. In short, attempting to mobilize the research resources of a university in order to attack urban (or other) problems, even if solving the urban problems were possible, might extract a price greater than the good achieved. But in view of the depth of urban problems, which go so much further than the cities, the little good which "the" university might accomplish, hardly seems to make worthwhile the distortions required to mobilize it, an institution neither designed nor accustomed to operate as a unified research center.

Government, foundation and industry research should be accepted by the university only if it serves an essential educational purpose or is otherwise related to the educational enterprise of the university and only if it can be accommodated without adversely affecting other more important university functions. The research project must serve the purposes of the university and not help to dilute its energies, its objectives, its personnel and its resources. The distinctive quality of a university is not that it has the capacity to be of service to the community, to the government, or to business, but rather that its service is to all these by virtue of its capacity as the place where objective scholarship and excellence are regarded as the criterion for admission and status.

On this question of research, I think it fair to say that student demands for greater time on the part of their instructors, greater visibility for the distinguished teachers and less isolation between funded researchers and the university are legitimate demands and demands which not only can be readily accommodated but must be accommodated if the university is to survive as an entity committed to the goal which I have identified as central—objective scholarship and teaching.

The connection between this last demand and the revitalization of undergraduate instruction is clear. It is not difficult to appreciate demands for improved instruction at the undergraduate level where the student is regarded as a necessary evil and time devoted to his instruction as an intrusion into the more important commitment to research. It may be that for some professors their research is more important to the university as a whole, but the glorification of research and its reward within the university have clearly been exaggerated. There are other reasons for the inadequacy of undergraduate education. One possible solution (and one which I believe President Nixon's administration will advance) is the development of the community college, where the sole commitment will be to the teaching of undergraduates.

More important, however, is the creation of a system of universities and colleges which do not all conceive of themselves as necessarily committed to the Harvard-Yale model. There is so much room for experimentation and yet so little experimentation.[54] The Harvard-Yale model has been so successful that innovations appear as heresy. The Harvard-Yale schools succeed largely because they accommodate only a certain type of student; they are not in the mass education business. I see nothing wrong with a college, e.g., committed to the views of the most extreme SDS membership: a college in which the students completely determine the program, where there are no grades, where militancy is encouraged, where revolutionary ideals are fostered, where students instruct the instructors, where there is no distinction between instructor and student, where courses are ungraded, unstructured, unprogrammed, where there is no regulation of student lives and no university housing and all the rest of whatever could be the most extreme demand of a most extreme SDS commitment. It seems to me universities ought to accommodate those students, and perhaps we have been mistaken in thinking students require a more disciplined environment in order to aim for worthy objectives. But to accommodate these students does not require denying the needs of students who do want their institution committed to objective scholarship, teaching and the tradition of excellence.

Much more difficult because they are not directed at the institution as it now exists but at notions of what it ought to be are the reforms of the institution, the demands for democratization.[55] Here the issues are very different because the objectives raise questions about the distinction between excellence and democratization. The demand for a contiguity admission policy, i.e., admitting all persons who live within a certain area in relation to the university, and the abandonment of standards for admission, as well as the demand for special programs and special institutes designed to meet the needs of adults who could not otherwise qualify for university programs but who have legitimate learning objectives—all of these are demands worthy of the most critical, most serious deliberation. Often they are demands which can be accommodated—but not within the structure of the universities as we now know them. So again there is a legitimate reason for arguing in favor of new kinds of educational experiences. But to ask that the universities abandon the job which they can do in order to satisfy these new needs, seems to me to raise a rather different kind of problem.

Many of the demands for self-determination by students are wholly compatible with institutions still committed to the general traditions of excellence. There are many places in which student participation would contribute to the excellence of the universities, would not frustrate the objectives of scholarship and teaching and would be compatible with the legitimate demands of students to be heard on matters on which they have some competence and interest. This is to be differentiated from a demand that the student is to be the primary source of decision on matters heretofore reserved for the senior faculty. It seems to me this explains the reason for the resignation of Mr. Rosstov in connection with the Black Studies program at Harvard. He, I suppose, would not be seriously disturbed were an entity established outside of Harvard to sponsor a program of such studies, but when the university wants to sponsor a Black Studies program then his objection seems to me well founded. To now bestow upon the students the critical determination for this one special program because of student pressure is an abandonment of very important principles. I thought it would take more than this to force Harvard to capitulate. Perhaps it was atoning for Mr. Pusey's use of the police.[56] But whatever the explanation, democratization of programs within the existing university structures is not compatible with the demands for excellence, teaching and objective scholarship.

I conclude by making five generalizations. The *first generalization* concerns the two demands left for last, because they cut across many different levels and raise a host of problems. I think Bayard Rustin [57] is correct in his observation about Black Studies programs generally, and particularly where they are subject to the further process of democratization which involves permitting black students to determine the quality of the courses given, the instruction, and the administrative relationship to the university. I think he is right in recognizing that Black Studies programs may be a hoax, a fraud utilized to obscure legitimate black demands. A Black Studies program need not be any different from an Asian or a South American Studies program. The question is not the area of study but the relationship between that area of study and the university programs as a whole. If a Black Studies program is to be structured, administered, taught and made subject to standards and criteria no different than those of the History Department or the Asian Studies Department, I see no special problem about Black Studies. But the issue of Black Studies has instead been used as a vehicle to raise demands for democratization, not for enlargement of the curriculum. Black Studies could be only an internal adjustment of curriculum or a serious demand for democratization within the existing structure. I would resist it on the latter and encourage it on the former.

I have left for last the questions of relevance and morality which seem to underlie so much of the student demand, and for this, let me go to what I would like to call a *second generalization:* The basic, underlying motif of the contemporary campus crisis *is* principled and philosophic. Students are rightly responding to the illusion of affluence and to the realization that there must be more to life than the now realizable goals of a chicken in every pot and a car in every garage. And what is more, to the extent to which students are moral protestants, education has succeeded. Learned Hand was so right when he said,

> Our dangers . . . are not from the outrageous but from the conforming; not from those who rarely and under the lurid glare of obliquy upset our moral complaisance, or shock us with unaccustomed conduct, but from those, the mass of us, who take their virtues and their tastes, like their shirts and their furniture, from the limited patterns which the market offers.[58]

Denied access to power or even to the learned journals, it seems to me that activist students are saying the very things which take up space in these journals. That is, we are becoming the victims of elitist power manipulators who control the new technologies and whose goals are advanced by repressing forms of fulfillment inimical to their interests. So, when students cry out for a humane world and demand that they not be treated like IBM cards, they are only echoing the deepest fears of older intellectuals. That they articulate these sentiments so badly is hardly the point.

What the student protestants mean when they demand relevance in education is that they want their education to be humane and relevant to the struggle against an increasingly amoral, mechanistic environment where human values appear to be losing ground in the struggle for material affluence. Surely, this demand must be capable of accommodation by the universities. The danger, however, is confusion on what constitutes relevance. Where short-sighted, hostile or immature students demand relevance, they often appear to mean not relevance as described above, but rather relevance in the sense of "useful" or "practical" or "contemporary." But even the professional schools must not be relevant in this sense. These schools would not serve their professions if they failed to develop their programs around the more enduring theoretical constructs which constitute the core identification of the profession. To teach lawyers how to win in court, but nothing about the meaning of justice, or to teach them how to enforce the obligations created by an installment sales contract, but nothing about the meaning of obligations, may well make their training relevant in the sense of useful, but it would certainly be antithetical to a relevant education as described above. To allow lawyers, doctors or businessmen or even mathematicians and Greek scholars, to leave the university equipped with the training and credentials which will enable them to earn a living off the cities (either directly, by practicing there, or indirectly, by working in an institution sustained by public taxes) is in itself not objectionable. It becomes objectionable—indeed obscene, when these same people are able to live off the cities without even being aware of the problems there, let alone doing anything about them. An education which permits this latter condition is rightly attacked as being irrelevant.

I make a *third generalization:* Because the discontent which underlies much student activism is justified, despite its nebulousness and precisely because student [59] activists are the successful product of an educational enterprise committed to the humane and liberal values of excellence and toleration, we must do two things: We must not destroy these successful students and these successful universities.

A *fourth generalization:* Existing universities can be responsive to the justifiable basis for activism and even accommodate many of the demands, and new universities can accommodate more radical changes, so long as the fascists of the left or right are not accommodated. Further, the universities must decide for themselves what constitutes an accommodation to fascism and not be legislated into such an accommodation. An unarmed George Wallace at the classroom door may be more of a fascist threat than an armed black student barricaded inside a campus building. And a foundation project-funder may be more dangerous than both.

And a *fifth and final generalization:* In order for the universities to decide for themselves what constitutes an accommodation to fascism and abandonment of the liberal virtues of toleration and excellence in university education, they must recapture the loyalty of their faculty. They must realize that the one ideology which is not tolerable is fascism from either side, and they must develop democratic procedures for the toleration and encouragement of dissent and the suppression of fascistic absolutism. The paradox for the universities has been this: They have been so committed to the liberal virtues, especially tolerance, that they have been unwilling to admit any dogmatism, even the dogmatic rejection of procedural fascism.

I believe that the universities were right to reject even this dogmatism because its acceptance means punishing young people who have not yet learned that the price of procedural fascism is substantive fascism. Too much is at stake to take the simplistic solution of throwing these students out of the universities, thus permanently depriving them of whatever the university has to offer. After all, these same young people agree with their professors on one score: If the university does no more than produce another set of IBM-card automatons every spring, we all lose.

Appendix I

From *The South End,* Vol. 26, No. 27 (Nov. 1, 1968); front page, "Protest Pig Riots Today."

The war between the people and the police was escalated Wednesday night as squads of hate crazed pigs brutally attacked hundreds of anti-Wallace demonstrators. With clubs swinging, mace spraying, and boots kicking, the pigs cracked heads, broke bones, bruised and battered men and women alike. It was the spectre of coming events, and a clear warning to Black and progressive Whites; the cops are killers, and the rise of the fascist rightwing, led by George Wallace, has given them the courage to show their most vicious, reactionary colors. Detroit witnessed another full fledged Pig Riot.

Let there be no mistake, the pigs were on George Wallace's side last Wednesday; they are on his side today, and they will remain on his side until the forces of revolution destroy them as a threat to safety in this society. . . .

The pro-Wallace crowd started the violence by spraying the demonstrators with a form of tear gas and hurling chairs at them. When the demonstrators properly defended themselves from the attacks, the pigs entered the fracas on the side of the fascists. One witness reported six pigs beating and kicking one man on the balcony of Cobo Hall. Other reports include the pigs handcuffing and holding anti-Wallace demonstrators and the pro-Wallace fascists beating them. . . .

The insane and brutal attack of the mad dog police against the anti-Wallace demonstrators was only the most recent of the ongoing history of atrocities committed by the pigs. Last month racist demented fascist Hamtramck dogs launched a frenzied ax handle and mace attack against the revolutionary Black workers of DRUM. The pigs attacked the Poor Peoples' March here in Detroit a few months ago. They make a regular habit of brutalizing Black high school students, and killing Black people is regular sport. Nobody knows how many Black people they murdered during the uprising in July, 1967, but for that matter, nobody knows how many they have killed since then.

Appendix II

The data presented below is based upon the survey of Wayne students conducted under the direction of Dr. Elliot Luby and me. The data include the test instrument and a table in percentages.

The interviews of law students were conducted by persons from outside the Law School. The other interviews were conducted by Senior law students who were taking the seminar on law and psychiatry taught jointly by Dr. Luby and me. These students also helped design the test instrument. Dr. Luby and I are pleased to have this occasion to express our appreciation for the exceptional work done by these students. They are: Raymond Converse, Stephen Cooper, Ray Delany, Robert Domol, William Kohne, Stephen Lea, James LeBlanc, Michael Pianin, Robert Roether, Sidney Suo, Michael Walsh, Mark Weiss, and Michael Weiss.

At the time of the survey (March to May 1969), there were 829 students in the Law School survey population, of which 73 were interviewed. There were 831 in Monteith College, of which 77 were interviewed, and there were 9880 in the College of Liberal Arts, of which 186 were interviewed. Only full-time students in the day schools were included in the relevant population. Monteith is an experimental liberal arts college where there is greater emphasis upon a humanities and social approach. Its students are more selectively admitted and they are supposedly more inclined towards a politics left of center.

The list of the students selected for interview was derived by taking, for the Law School and Monteith, every twentieth name on the roster and every fiftieth name for the Liberal Arts college.

The Test Instrument

Questionnaire on Student-University Relationship

SECTION I: *Demographic Background*
1. Age
2. Sex
3. Living alone or at home
4. How many hours do you work per week
5. Approximately how much do you earn per week during the school year
6. Do your parents contribute significantly to your college education
7. Race
8. Marital status
9. Military Service. How long and where
10. What is your present Selective Service classification
11. Where were you born and raised
12. What is the general socio-economic status of your parents Would you say they are wealthy, upper middle class, lower middle class, poor
13. What is your major
14. In which college are you presently a student
15. What year are you
16. Were you raised by both your parents until you reached the age of approximately 16 or 17. If raised by only one, which one
17. What is your religious preference, if any

18. Are you politically active. If yes, for which party
19. What is your honor-point average

SECTION II: *General Attitudes*

1. What do you think about the war in Vietnam? Are you generally for it or against it? How would you rank your attitude towards this war on a scale ranging from say one to five where one is strongly for and five is strongly opposed?
2. What do you think about the general behavior of the police? On a scale ranging from one to five, how would you rank your attitude where one represents the view that you generally think police behave helpfully and are protective, to five which would represent the view that you think the police generally behave in a vicious and brutal manner
3. On a scale ranging from one to five, where one represents the view that black people should stop rioting and start behaving and five represents the view that they ought to act violently and overthrow the government, how do you think black people should act
4. Do you tend to think that voting in a national or state election is likely to be a waste of time because the Establishment has already pretty well determined what is going to happen regardless of your vote?
5. If the federal government was in the process of preparing legislation which you know will affect you, what would you do, if anything, if you wished to affect that proposed legislation?

SECTION III: *Attitudes Toward the University*

1. Why are you going to a University?
2. Why are you going to Wayne?
3. Do you think you are receiving a good education at Wayne?
4. Do you think you are receiving a relevant education at Wayne?
5. In general, how do you feel about Wayne? How would you rank the University on a scale of from one to five,

191

where one might represent the feeling that Wayne is a great University, to five, which might represent the view that it is pretty much a waste of time to be here?

6. In general, do you think the University administration is responsive to the needs of students? On a scale of from one to five, where one represents generally responsive to three which might be apathetic, to five which might be antagonistic, how would you rank the University on this matter?

7. Who do you think really runs this University?
    a. Campus Police
    b. Mr. Keast, Mr. Cushman and their group of close administrative associates
    c. The Faculty
    d. Mr. Keast
    e. The Students
    f. Mr. Cushman
    g. The Board of Governors
    h. Some other? If other, which other?

8. a. Do you think the University deals fairly with students who come in conflict with the University?
    b. Do you think the University is concerned with protecting their legitimate rights when there is some conflict?

SECTION IV: *Student Power*

1. Are you now or have you ever been active in any University sponsored or approved groups?
    a. Social
    b. Concerned with the governance of students or student-faculty
    c. Athletic
    d. Political
    e. Professional
    f. Honorary
    g. Other

2. Do you think the administration of the University can be influenced by students, through:
    a. University groups
    b. Extra University groups
    c. Not at all

3. Have you ever participated in a peaceful demonstration?

4. Have you ever participated in:
    a. Picketing
    b. Petitioning
    c. A sit-in
    d. Marching
    e. Some other form of demonstration
5. Have you ever participated in:
    a. A violent demonstration on campus
    b. A violent demonstration off campus
6. If the University wishes to suspend or expel a student for cause, do you think the student is entitled to have a hearing?
7. If the student is entitled to a hearing, should the hearing panel be composed of:
    a. All students
    b. All faculty
    c. Students-Faculty
    d. Faculty administrators
    e. Some other combination
8. Would you attend a credit course taught by:
    a. Stokely Carmichael
    b. a John Bircher
9. Should students have a significant voice in:
    a. The hiring of new personnel
    b. The granting of tenure to existing faculty
    c. The discharge of a faculty man
    d. In curriculum planning
    e. Other areas. If so, where
10. Do you read The South End, the campus newspaper, fairly regularly?
11. Do you think The South End is:
    a. Well-written
    b. Interesting
12. Do you think The South End represents:
    a. A significant part of the University students
    b. An insignificant part
    c. Only the black students
    d. Probably only a small per cent of the black students
    e. Some other. If so, what
13. Do you think The South End:

193

      a. Devotes too much space to University sports and social events

      b. Should devote more space to these matters

14. Do you think the editor of The South End should be elected:
    a. By the outgoing editorial Board of students
    b. By a special student-faculty committee
    c. By a special faculty committee
    d. Other. If other, what

15. Do you think it would be wrong for the University to require the editors of The South End to withdraw or alter an item in the newspaper, if, before its publication, they knew that the item would:
    a. Use on the front page in large letters an extremely objectionable obscenity
    b. Urge students to throw rotten tomatoes and eggs at a presidential candidate
    c. Urge students to block access to the President's or some other University administrator's private residence
    d. Urge students to pursue a clearly illegal course of conduct

16. How would you act if you heard of plans for a demonstration protesting:

    16.1   Job interviewers from a defense oriented company on campus:
          a. I would condone or sympathize
          b. Participate
          c. Try to make the demonstration violent
          d. NOT condone or sympathize
          e. NOT participate
          f. I would not give a damn
          g. Counter-demonstrate

    16.2   University disciplinary action against staff members or editors of student paper because of an editorial

    16.3   University disciplinary action against elected student leaders

    16.4   Expansion of the University onto lands now inner-city residential

    16.5   Involvement of the U.S. in Vietnam

    16.6   The Military Draft

16.7   The use of napalm bombing

16.8   The use of soldiers in patrolling city streets

16.9   The existence of University Police Department

16.10 University police carrying firearms

16.11 University police's file of subversive students

16.12 University police's file of students' sexual activities

17. How would you act if you heard of plans for a demonstration *in support of:*

    17.1   Black Power

        a. I would condone or sympathize

        b. Participate

        c. Try to make the demonstration violent

        d. NOT condone nor sympathize

        e. NOT participate

        f. I would not give a damn

        g. Counter-demonstrate

    17.2   A particular political candidate

    17.3   Expanding aid to welfare participants

    17.4   Increased student influence

    17.5   Increased student influence in planning curriculum

18. Do you think the University should be allowed to discipline or expel students who engage in certain activities? The question is not "Should the University" but "Should the University be allowed to"

A Student Who . . .

    18.1   Cheats on a test

        a. Discipline only

        b. Expulsion only

        c. Both

        d. Neither

    18.2   Fails to do his assignments for class

    18.3   Does not attend classes

    18.4   Insults a professor or University staff member

    18.5   Insults the University president

    18.6   Joins an organization not sanctioned by the University

    18.7   Is arrested for nonpayment of traffic tickets on campus

    18.8   Is arrested for a sit-in demonstration

    18.9   Is arrested for possession of marijuana

    18.10 Is arrested for an unlawful sexual act

18.11 Is arrested for commission of a robbery

18.12 Posed nude for the Playboy centerfold

18.13 Was convicted for commission of a robbery

18.14 Was convicted for commission of an unlawful sexual act

19. How would you act, if after the usual machinery (e.g., appeals through channels, etc.) had failed, and the University were to:

19.1 Pursue educational objectives which you thought immoral and improper

    a. Do nothing

    b. Write a letter. If so, to whom

    c. Sign a petition

    d. Join organized picketing

    e. Join organized boycotts of classes

    f. Join organized sit-in not designed to disrupt University functions

    g. Join organized sit-in designed to disrupt University functions

    h. Seize the University

    i. Burn University research records and files

    j. Demonstrate against the demonstrators

    k. Other. If so, what

19.2 Pursue a social policy which you thought immoral and improper

19.3 Pursue a fiscal policy which you thought immoral and improper

19.4 Pursue a policy which permitted George Wallace to speak on campus

19.5 Pursue a policy which permitted Eldridge Cleaver to speak on campus

19.6 Allow job interviews on campus by war-oriented corporations

19.7 Pursue a policy of allowing war-related research

20. What kind of essentially campus-centered conduct would you be willing to engage in, in order to protest:

20.1 Federal draft policy

    (Alternatives as in 19.1)

20.2 Federal war policy

20.3 Federal poverty program

20.4   Federal drug laws

20.5   Federal obscenity laws

21. If the South End represents only a small part of the campus community and even if it were to be representative of only a small part of the community served by Wayne, do you think the University should continue to support its activities because:

   a. It is educating the campus community as to an important contemporary matter.
   b. It is presenting and defending a position which deserves to be heard on campus.
   c. The editor and staff in their exercise of the right of free speech may do whatever they think best with the paper—subject only to the constitution itself.
   d. For some other reason. If so what?
   e. It ought not be further supported by the University.

The Table

In the table reference to the test instrument is necessary. Please note that the instrument is divided into four sections, identified by roman numerals, and that the questions within each section, in arabic numerals, begin with the number 1. Thus, IV, 8 refers to the question on a credit course taught by a) Stokely Carmichael, b) a John Bircher.

The figures in the table are percentages. Thus, in Section IV, 8a, of all those interviewed, 52.7 percent in the College of Liberal Arts answered the question in the affirmative, 72.7 percent in Monteith, and 61.6 percent in the Law School. The full data on which the percentages are based is available.

SECTION I—*Demographic Background*

	Lib. Arts	Monteith	Law
	%	%	%
1. Age (18–20 yrs.)	69	69	71
2. Male	56	52	94.5
Female	44	48	4.1
3. Living alone	19	25	26
Living at home	70	65	34
Married	11	10	40
4. Work 0 hours per week	38	40	55
Work 10 or less hours per week	11	7.8	16.4
Work 30 or more hours per week	11	10.4	5.5
5. Earn nothing	37	44	55
6. Parents do contribute significantly	57	52	45
Parents do not contribute significantly	43	48	55
7. White	90	96	100
Black	10	4	0
Oriental	.5	0	0
8. Single	87	87	50.7
Married	11	10.4	48
9. Omitted			
10. Draft status 2-S	40	30	27.4
11. Born in Detroit or Detroit metropolitan area	83	78	39.7
Raised in Detroit or Detroit metropolitan area	89	87	46.6
12. All respondents			
Wealthy	1.6	2.6	5.5
Upper middle class	44.6	46.7	61.6
Lower middle class	35	26	30
Poor	2.7	1.3	0
Middle middle class	15.6	22	2.7
12. Black respondents only			
Wealthy	None–0		
Upper middle class	2–22		
Lower middle class	11–61		
Poor	2–11		
Middle middle class	1–6		

	Lib. Arts %	Monteith %	Law %
13. Omitted			
14. Omitted			
15. Omitted			
16. Raised by both parents	86.5	80.5	97
17. Religious preferences			
Catholic	43	24.7	13.7
Protestant	21.5	20.8	34
Jewish	9	13	24.7
None	22.5	35	26
18. Politically active respondents	16	21	30
Active as Democratic	10	6.5	12.3
Active as Republican	1.6	3.9	12.3
Active Independent		3.9	4.1

SECTION II—*General Attitudes*

	Lib. Arts	Monteith	Law
1. War in Viet Nam generally opposed (respondents answering 4 or 5)	70	78	74
2. Police behavior generally helpful (respondents answering 2 or 3)	74	58	83.6
3. Behavior of black people—should stop rioting (respondents answering 2 or 3)	67	61	71
4. Voting is a waste of time	38.7	36	19
Voting is not a waste of time	60	58	80.8
5. Should write to a Congressman	60	56	85

SECTION III—*Attitudes Toward the University*

	Lib. Arts	Monteith	Law
1. Attending university to get a degree	56.5	60	41.1
Attending university to have a profession and job	26	21	32.9
Attending university for economic reasons	6	2.6	11
2. Attending Wayne because a good school	14.5	13	17.8
Attending Wayne because near home	54	40	28.8

	Lib. Arts %	Monteith %	Law %
Attending Wayne for financial reasons	17	17	13.7
3. Getting a good education at Wayne	87	83	94.5
Not getting a good education at Wayne	8.6	10	5.5
4. Getting a relevant education at Wayne	76	82	82.2
Not getting a relevant education at Wayne	18	17	15.1
5. That Wayne is pretty good	77.4	76.6	84.9
6. Administration at Wayne rather apathetic to students (respondents answering 2 or 3)	80.6	63.6	82.2
7. Who really runs Wayne?			
a. Police	1.1	0	0
b. Keast and top administrators	36	36	47.9
c. Faculty	7	3.4	13.7
d. Keast	5	3.4	9.6
e. Students	3	1.3	17.8
f. Cushman	24	0	1.4
g. Board of Governors	6.5	24.7	5.5
8. a. Believe university generally fair with students	61	58	63

SECTION IV—*Student Power*

	Lib. Arts %	Monteith %	Law %
1. Not active in university sponsored or approved groups	60.7	59.7	23
a. Active in such social groups	17	9.1	37
b. Active in student government groups	1.6	9.1	5.5
c. Active in such athletic groups	4.3	5.2	8.2
d. Active in such political groups	4.3	6.5	6.8
e. Active in such professional groups	4.3	3.4	5.5
2. a. Believe university administration can be influenced by university groups	54	45.5	43.8

	Lib. Arts %	Monteith %	Law %
b. Believe university can be influenced by extra university groups	13	15.6	5.5
c. Believe university cannot be influenced at all	7.5	9.1	4
3. Have participated in peaceful demonstration	34	54.5	32.9
Have not participated in peaceful demonstration	65	44	67
4. a. Participated in picketing	7	9.1	15.1
b. In petitioning	24	24.7	42.5
c. In a sit-in	2.7	3.9	0
d. In marching	5.4	15.6	0
5. a. Have participated in violent demonstrations on campus	1.07	3.9	0
a. Have not participated in violent demonstrations on campus	97.8	94.8	100
b. Have participated in violent demonstrations off campus	3.2	9.1	8.2
b. Have not participated in violent demonstrations off campus	95.7	88.3	91.8
6. Omitted			
7. a. Hearing panel should be all students	4.8	9.1	1.4
c. Hearing panel should be students-faculty	68	65	52.1
8. a. Would attend credit course by Carmichael	52.7	72.7	61.6
a. Would not attend such course	44.6	24.7	37
b. Would attend credit course by Bircher	39.2	58.4	46.6
b. Would not attend such course	58.6	39	53.4
9. a. Students should have voice in hiring personnel	37.6	59.7	31.5

	Lib. Arts %	Monteith %	Law %
b. Students should have voice on tenure	53	66	60.1
c. Students should have voice on discharge	67	75	53
d. Students should have voice on curriculum	86	93.5	83.6
10. Do you read South End fairly regularly?	64.5	72.7	58.9
Do not read South End fairly regularly?	33.9	26	39.7
11. a. Believe South End well written	16.6	28.6	13.7
b. Believe South End interesting	50	72.7	50.7
12. b. Believe South End represents insignificant part of students	44.6	29.9	49.3
d. Believe South End represents small percent of black students	26.9	28.6	32.9
13. a. Believe South End should give more sports and social coverage	70	31.2	56.2
14. a. Think South End editor should be named by student editorial board	18	24.7	17.8
b. Should be named by special student faculty committee	56	45.5	56.2
c. Should be named by special faculty committee	7.5	2.6	8.2
15. Not wrong for university to censor:			
a. Obscenity	48	37.7	38.4
b. For abuse of presidential candidate	49	45.5	45
c. For urging direct action against university president	49	33.7	43.8
d. For urging direct action which entailed illegal conduct	44	39	42.5

	Lib. Arts %	Monteith %	Law %
16.1 b. Would participate in demonstration against campus interviews by defense company	11	15.6	1.4
c. Would try to make demonstration violent	0	0	0
e. Would not participate in demonstration	27	24.7	30
16.2 b. Would participate in demonstration on student newspaper	18.8	35.1	11
c. Would try to make demonstration violent	.53	0	1.4
e. Would not try to make demonstration violent	23.7	16.9	22
16.3 b. Would participate in demonstration about student leaders	25	39	20.5
c. Would try to make demonstration violent	0	1.3	0
e. Would not participate	17.7	14.3	22
16.4 b. Would participate in demonstration about university expansion	17.7	32.5	4
c. Would try to make demonstration violent	.53	0	0
e. Would not participate	226	19.5	30
16.5 b. Would participate in demonstration against Viet Nam War	30.6	42.6	23.3
c. Would try to make demonstration violent	0	1.29	2.7
e. Would not participate	19	16.9	23.3
16.6 b. Would participate in demonstration against draft	35	44	11
c. Would try to make demonstration violent	0	2.59	1.4
e. Would not participate	21.5	15.6	23.3
16.7 b. Would participate in demonstration against napalm bombing	28.5	49.4	6.8

	Lib. Arts %	Monteith %	Law %
c. Would try to make demonstration violent	0	2.6	1.4
e. Would not participate	21.5	14.3	26
16.8 b. Would participate in demonstration against soldiers on streets	23.7	42.6	9.6
c. Would try to make demonstration violent	0	0	1.4
e. Would not participate	23	13	20.5
16.9 b. Would participate in demonstration against existence of university police	6.5	11.7	2.7
c. Would try to make demonstration violent	0	0	0
e. Would not participate	30	28.6	26
16.10 b. Would participate in demonstration against university police with firearms	16	20.8	5.5
c. Would try to make demonstration violent	.53	1.3	0
e. Would not participate	25	20.8	26
16.11 b. Would participate in demonstration against university police's file on subversive students	20	37.7	15.1
c. Would try to make demonstration violent	0	1.3	1.4
e. Would not participate	21	14.3	16.4
16.12 b. Would participate in demonstration against university police's file on student sex conduct	30	44	19.2
c. Would try to make demonstration violent	0	3.9	4
e. Would not participate	16.7	9.1	8
17.1 b. Would participate in demonstration supporting black power	11.3	9.1	2.7
c. Would try to make demonstration violent	.53	0	1.4

		Lib. Arts %	Monteith %	Law %
	e. Would not participate	35	16.9	32.9
17.2	b. Would participate in demonstration supporting particular political candidate	42.5	35.1	45
	c. Would try to make demonstration violent	0	0	0
	e. Would not participate	11.3	15.6	4
17.3	b. Would participate in demonstration supporting expanded aid to welfare	21	20.8	4
	c. Would try to make demonstration violent	0	0	0
	e. Would not participate	17	14.3	23
17.4	b. Would participate in demonstration supporting increased student influence	35	44.2	13.7
	c. Would try to make demonstration violent	0	0	0
	e. Would not participate	11.3	7.8	16
17.5	b. Would participate in demonstration supporting student influence on curriculum	45.7	57	22
	c. Would try to make demonstration violent	0	0	1.4
	e. Would not participate	9	5.2	9.6
18.	Would you allow the university to discipline or expel students:			
18.1	Who cheat on a test			
	a. Discipline only	59	66	45
	b. Expulsion only	6	4	6
	d. Neither	18	14	1
18.2	Who fails to do his assignments for class			
	a. Discipline only	34	31	40
	b. Expulsion only	.5	1	0
	d. Neither	64.5	66	56
18.3	Does not attend classes			
	a. Discipline only	26	15.6	27

205

	Lib. Arts %	Monteith %	Law %
b. Expulsion only	2	0	0
d. Neither	66	79	64
18.4 Insults a professor or University staff member			
a. Discipline only	47	30	48
b. Expulsion only	3	4	0
d. Neither	42	60	34
18.5 Insults the University president			
a. Discipline only	39	27	47
b. Expulsion only	4	5	1
d. Neither	46	61	41
18.6 Joins an organization not sanctioned by University			
a. Discipline only	11	5	8
b. Expulsion only	2	0	0
d. Neither	85.5	90	90
18.7 Is arrested for nonpayment of traffic tickets on campus			
a. Discipline only	22.6	15.6	23
b. Expulsion only	0	0	0
d. Neither	1	83	74
18.8 Is arrested for a sit-in demonstration			
a. Discipline only	76	8	16
b. Expulsion only	26	0	3
d. Neither	1	86	73
18.9 Is arrested for possession of marijuana			
a. Discipline only	17	8	8
b. Expulsion only	9	2.6	7
d. Neither	64.5	80.5	64
18.10 Is arrested for an unlawful sexual act			
a. Discipline only	12	2.6	4
b. Expulsion only	6	3.4	4
d. Neither	74	88	79.5
18.11 Is arrested for commission of a robbery			
a. Discipline only	16	13	4

	Lib. Arts %	Monteith %	Law %
b. Expulsion only	8	2.6	11
d. Neither	68	80.5	68.5
18.12 Posed nude for the Playboy centerfold			
a. Discipline only	8	1	4
b. Expulsion only	2	0	0
d. Neither	85	97	69
18.13 Was convicted for commission of a robbery			
a. Discipline only	10	8	3
b. Expulsion only	14	10	14
d. Neither	57.5	72	52
18.14 Was convicted for commission of an unlawful sexual act			
a. Discipline only	10	6.5	4
b. Expulsion only	9	9	8
d. Neither	62	74	63
19. How would you act if after every established method of objection had failed, the university were to:			
19.1 Pursue educational objectives you consider immoral and improper			
a. Do nothing	7	8	4
d. Join organized picketing	7.5	8	7
e. Join organized boycotts of classes	19	26	12
g. Join organized sit-in designed to disrupt University functions	6.5	10	3
h. Seize the University	1	1	1
19.2 Pursue social policy you consider immoral and improper			
a. Do nothing	14.5	10	14
d. Join organized picketing	11	13	9.6
e. Join organized boycotts of classes	7.5	13	7

		Lib. Arts %	Monteith %	Law %
	g. Join organized sit-in designed to disrupt University functions	7	13	0
	h. Seize the University	1	1	1
19.3	Pursue fiscal policy you consider immoral and improper			
	a. Do nothing	13	14	15
	d. Join organized picketing	10	10	4
	e. Join organized boycotts of classes	6.5	14	5.5
	g. Join organized sit-in designed to disrupt University functions	5	4	0
	h. Seize the University	1	4	1
19.4	Pursue policy which permitted George Wallace to speak on campus			
	a. Do nothing	79	84	97
	d. Join organized picketing	5	5	0
	e. Join organized boycotts of classes	2	1	0
	g. Join organized sit-in designed to disrupt University functions	1	1	0
	h. Seize the University	1	0	0
19.5	Pursue policy which permitted Eldridge Cleaver to speak on campus			
	a. Do nothing	82	83	97
	d. Join organized picketing	2	4	0
	e. Join organized boycotts of classes	2	0	0
	g. Join organized sit-in designed to disrupt University functions	.5	1	0
	h. Seize the University	1	0	0
19.6	Allow job interviews on campus by war-oriented corporations			
	a. Do nothing	66	57	82

		Lib. Arts %	*Monteith* %	*Law* %
	d. Join organized picketing	6.5	13	3
	e. Join organized boycotts of classes	3	2.6	0
	g. Join organized sit-in designed to disrupt University functions	3	2.6	0
	h. Seize the University	.5	0	1
19.7	Pursue policy of allowing war-related research			
	a. Do nothing	49	38	73
	d. Join organized picketing	11	13	3
	e. Join organized boycotts of classes	2	6.5	0
	g. Join organized sit-in designed to disrupt University functions	2	9	0
	h. Seize the University	.5	1	1
20.	What would you be willing to protest as a campus centered activity?:			
20.1	Federal draft policy			
	a. Do nothing	17	14	16
	d. Join organized picketing	16	19	12
	e. Join organized boycotts of classes	5	12	3
	g. Join organized sit-in designed to disrupt University functions	5	5	1
	h. Seize the University	0	1	0
20.2	Federal war policy			
	a. Do nothing	17	13	19
	d. Join organized picketing	17	23	14
	e. Join organized boycotts of classes	5	9	3
	g. Join organized sit-in designed to disrupt University functions	5	6.5	1
	h. Seize the University	.5	1	1
20.3	Federal poverty program			
	a. Do nothing	28	25	31.5

		Lib. Arts %	Monteith %	Law %
	d. Join organized picketing	11	8	15
	e. Join organized boycotts of classes	3	5	0
	g. Join organized sit-in designed to disrupt University functions	2	2.6	0
	h. Seize the University	0	0	0
20.4	Federal drug laws			
	a. Do nothing	36	26	33
	d. Join organized picketing	11	17	7
	e. Join organized boycotts of classes	3	4	0
	g. Join organized sit-in designed to disrupt University functions	1	26	0
	h. Seize the University	0	0	0
20.5	Federal obscenity laws			
	a. Do nothing	39	31	36
	d. Join organized picketing	9	13	10
	e. Join organized boycotts of classes	3	1	1
	g. Join organized sit-in designed to disrupt University functions	.5	0	0
	h. Seize the University	0	0	0
21.	a. University should support South End because educating campus community	5	8	5
	b. Should support South End because defending position which should be heard	21.5	32	14
	c. Should support South End on ground of free speech	15	23	22
	e. University ought not further support South End	42	17	55

Notes

Social Policy and Direct Action as Freedom of Expression

1. The concept of order is itself hardly a paradigm of order or clarity. See e.g., Kuntz, ed., *The Concept of Order* (1968), especially the section on "Order in Human Societies," 339–404 and particularly Friedrich, "The Dialectics of Political Order and Freedom," 339 ff. Professor Friedrich distinguishes four different understandings of what constitutes order; in only one of these, is peace the focal point.
2. Shuman, *Legal Positivism: Its Scope and Limitations* (1963), esp. Chap. I.
3. Fuller, *The Morality of Law* (1964), esp. Chap. II.
4. Hart, "Positivism and the Separation of Law and Morals," 71 *Harv. L. Rev.* 593 (1958) and Fuller, "Positivism and Fidelity to Law—A Reply to Professor Hart," 71 *Harv. L. Rev.* 630 (1958).
5. See Meikeljohn, *Free Speech and Its Relation to Self-Government* (1948).
6. *Abrams v. U. S.*, 250 U.S. 616 (1919).
7. Huntington, *Political Order in Changing Society* (1968).
8. For sources and citations relevant to this theory, see Vol. I. of Emerson, Haber and Dorsen, *Political and Civil Rights in the United States* (3rd ed., 1967).
9. *Shuttlesworth v. City of Birmingham*, 394 U.S. 147 (1969).
10. *Shuttlesworth*, at 151.
11. *Shuttlesworth*, quoting from *Jones v. City of Opelika*, 316 U.S. 584, 602 (1941).
12. 347 U.S. 483 (1954).
13. Deutsch, "Neutrality, Legitimacy and the Supreme Court: Some Intersections Between Law and Political Science," 20 *Stanford L. Rev.* 169, esp. 198 ff. (1968).

14. Cahn, "Justice Black and the First Amendment 'Absolutes': A Public Interview," 37 *N.Y.U. L. Rev.* 549 (1962).
15. Henkin, "Selective Incorporation in the Fourteenth Amendment," 73 *Yale L. J.* 74 (1963).
16. Kadish, "Methodology and Criteria in Due Process Adjudication—A Survey and Criticism," 66 *Yale L. J.* 319 (1958).
17. Nimer, "The Right to Speak from Time to Time: First Amendment Theory Applied to Libel and Misapplied to Privacy," 56 *Calif. L. Rev.* 935 (1968).
18. On some advantages of such a weighing technique, see e.g., Mendelson "On the Meaning of the First Amendment: Absolutes in the Balance," 50 *Calif. L. Rev.* 821 (1962). Also see Karst, "Legislative Facts in Constitutional Litigation," in Kurland, ed., *Supreme Court Rev.* 75 (1960). On the disadvantages of balancing on an ad hoc basis, see e.g., Emerson, "Towards a General Theory of First Amendment," 72 *Yale L. J.* 887 (1963). Also see Frantz, "The First Amendment in Balance," 71 *Yale L. J.* 424 (1962).
19. As between public order and free speech, "the duty of the courts is to determine which of these two conflicting interests demands the greater protection under the particular circumstances presented." *Am. Communications Association v. Douds,* 339 U.S. 382, 399 (1950).
20. *New York Times v. Sullivan,* 376 U.S. 255 (1964).
21. See e.g., Justice Frankfurter concurring in *Dennis v. United States,* 341 U.S. 494, 524 ff. (1951), and Justice Harlan in *Barenblatt v. United States,* 360 U.S. 109 (1959).
22. Nimer, supra Note 17 at 939 ff.
23. Nimer, supra Note 17 esp. 942 ff.
24. *New York Times v. Sullivan,* 376 U.S. 254 (1964); also see *Rosenblatt v. Baer,* 383 U.S. 75 (1966), and see the analysis of these cases in "The Supreme Court, 1965 Term," 80 *Harv. L. Rev.* 91, 194 ff. (1966).
25. *Curtis Publishing Co. v. Butts,* 388 U.S. 130 (1967); *Assoc. Press v. Walker,* 388 U.S. 130 (1967). According to the *Times* case, actual malice would seem to be required before the defendant loses the privilege of comment which in other circumstances would be libel. But in the later two cases, four justices seem to support the view that a public figure, not an official, might recover for a libel if there is "highly unreasonable conduct constituting an extreme departure from the standards of investigation and reporting ordinarily adhered to by responsible publishers." *Walker* at 155. See the analysis of these cases in "The Supreme Court, 1966 Term," 81 *Harv. L. Rev.* 69, 160 ff. (1967).
26. *Rosenblatt v. Baer,* supra Note 24 at 198 ff.

27. Ratner, "The Function of the Due Process Clause," 116 *U. Penn. L. Rev.* 1048 (1968).
28. Greenberg, "The Supreme Court, Civil Rights and Civil Dissonance," 77 *Yale L. J.* 1520 (1968).
29. 378 U.S. 347 (1964).
30. 394 U.S. 111 (1969).
31. Gregory, "Day in Court," *The South End,* the student newspaper of Wayne State University, Apr. 30, 1969, p. 2, col. 1.
32. Supra Note 30 at 118.
33. Rembar, *The End of Obscenity* (1968); *Ginzberg v. U.S.,* 383 U.S. 463 (1966); *Ginsberg v. New York,* 390 U.S. 629 (1968).
34. *Edwards v. South Carolina,* 372 U.S. 229 (1963).
35. *Feiner v. New York,* 340 U.S. 315 (1951).
36. 383 U.S. 131, 133 Note 1 (1966).
37. "Freedom of Speech and Assembly: The Problem of the Hostile Audience," 49 *Colum. L. Rev.,* 118 (1949); "Constitutional Law—Free Speech and the Hostile Audience," 26 *N.Y.U. L. Rev.* 489 (1951); Kalvin, *The Negro and the First Amendment,* esp. 140 ff. (1965).
38. 373 U.S. 284, esp. 293 ff. (1963).
39. 378 U.S. 146, esp. 150 ff. (1964).
40. See supra Note 24, at 154 ff. for an analysis of these cases; also see Kalvin, supra Note 37 at 216 ff.
41. Emerson, supra Note 18; "Symbolic Conduct," 68 *Colum. L. Rev.* 1091 (1968).
42. Subject to reasonable limitations, *Kovacs v. Cooper,* 336 U.S. 77 (1949); *Public Util. Commission v. Pollock,* 343 U.S. 451 (1952).
43. Emerson, supra Note 18 at 917.
44. *Brown v. Louisiana,* 383 U.S. 131, 141–2 (1966).
45. See e.g., Justice Harlan concurring in *Garner v. Louisiana,* 368 U.S. 157, 201 (1961).
46. *Stromberg v. California,* 283 U.S. 359, 632 (1931).
47. *West Virginia State Board of Education v. Barnett,* 319 U.S. 624 (1943).
48. However to the contrary, Justice Fortas in *Concerning Dissent and Civil Disobedience* (1968) says, "It is hardly likely that anyone would seriously contest" the constitutionality of prohibitions against flag desecration. For the judicial affirmation of this view, see the dissenting opinions (including one by Justice Fortas) but also consider the majority view in the just decided case of *Street v. New York* 398 U.S. 576 (1969). For an interesting, and I find convincing, criticism of the Justice for having written that book, see Baldwin, "Justice Fortas on Dissent and Civil Disobedience: Heretic or Hero?—A little of Both," *Wis. L. Rev.* 220 (1969).

49. That is, displaying such a flag may not be privileged in those circumstances any more than "fighting words" may be protected by the First Amendment.

50. *People v. Street,* 20 N.Y. 2d 231, 229 N.E. 2d 187 (1967). See also, "Symbolic Conduct," supra Note 41, 1103 ff. for an analysis of *People v. Street.* Since I wrote this, the conviction was reversed, but on highly technical grounds, which produced four dissenting opinions; see *Street v. New York,* supra Note 48.

51. *United States v. O'Brien,* 391 U.S. 376 (1968).

52. [However], *The Wall Street Journal* did seek to identify and analyze the kinds of interests which should be balanced. It said of "illegal acts like burning . . . draft cards or indulging in 'peaceful' marches," that:

> By now this variety of "free speech"—which is devoid of intellectual content, invites no debate, tolerates no rebuttal, trades on emotion, bases its appeal on sheer numbers of demonstrators and beckons to exploitation—has become so accepted it is employed on the slightest impulse by dissatisfied groups of every description. In our opinion, it cannot be too strongly emphasized that most of the street action is not an expression but a debasement of honest public discussion of the issues, Vietnam or anything else, and in fact of the whole Constitutional concept of free assembly.

53. For a very full analysis of this matter with references to much of the literature, see Deutsch, supra Note 13.

54. Shapiro, *Law and Politics in the Supreme Court: New Approaches to Political Jurisprudence* (1964).

55. See, e.g., *Edwards v. South Carolina,* supra Note 34; also, see *Brown v. Louisiana,* supra Note 44 at 146 ff.

56. *Brown v. Louisiana,* supra Note 44; also, see *Bell v. Maryland,* 378 U.S. 226 (1964).

57. *Giboney v. Empire Storage & Ice Co.,* 336 U.S. 490 (1949).

58. *Cox v. Louisiana I,* 379 U.S. 536, 555 (1965); *Cox v. Louisiana II,* 379 U.S. 559, 562 ff. (1965); *Edwards v. South Carolina,* supra Note 34.

59. *Adderley v. Florida,* 385 U.S. 39 (1966).

60. *Hague v. C.I.O.,* 307 U.S. 496 (1939) (park); *Schneider v. State,* 308 U.S. 147 (1939) (street); *Edwards v. South Carolina,* supra Note 34 (statehouse grounds).

61. See *Cox v. Louisiana I,* supra Note 58 at 574; *Poulos v. New Hampshire,* 345 U.S. 395, 405 (1953).

62. Supra Note 44, esp. at 166; note this same language in the opinion of Justice Fortas at 142.

63. *Food Employees Local 590 v. Logan Valley Plaza, Inc.,* 391 U.S. 308 (1968).

64. Supra Note 59 at 47.

65. Supra Note 63 at 325.

66. See "The Supreme Court, 1967 Term," 82 *Harv. L. Rev.* 63, 135 ff. (1968).

67. See "The Supreme Court, 1966 Term," supra Note 25 at 140 ff. (1967).

68. Ratner, supra Note 27.

69. McLuhan, *Understanding Media: the Extension of Man* (1964).

70. Barron, "Access to the Press—A New First Amendment Right," 80 *Harv. L. Rev.* 1641 (1967); "Symbolic Conduct," supra Note 41.

71. "Symbolic Conduct," supra Note 41 at 1091, Note 4.

72. For an analysis of these protests and the "content" of the message as distinguished from the affect of the protest, see generally, Finnan and Macaulay, "Freedom to Dissent: The Vietnam Protests and the Words of Public Officials," 1966 *Wis. L. Rev.* 632.

73. *Gregory v. Chicago,* supra Note 30 at 120, 125.

74. "Symbolic Conduct," supra Note 41 at 1109 ff.

75. See Kalvin, supra Note 37, esp. 123 ff.

76. *Tinker v. Des Moines Ind. Community School District,* 393 U.S. 503, (1969). Dissenting in this case, Justice Black states:

> One defying pupil was Paul Tinker, 8 years old, who was in the second grade; another, Hope Tinker was 11 years old in the fifth grade; a third member of the Tinker family was 13, in the eighth grade; and a fourth member of the same family was John Tinker, 15 years old, an 11th grade high school pupil. Their father, a Methodist minister without a church, is paid a salary by the American Friends Service Committee. Another student who defied the school order and insisted on wearing an armband in school was Chris Eckhardt, an 11th grade pupil and a petitioner in this case. His mother is an official in the Women's International League for Peace and Freedom. At 516.

77. Supra, Note 76 at 505 ff.

78. Fortas, supra Note 48.

79. Harrington, "Is America by Nature a Violent Society," *New York Times Magazine* 24, 111 (Apr. 28, 1968).

80. Arendt, "Reflections on Violence," 28 *J. Inter. Affairs 1* (1969).

81. De Tocqueville, *Democracy in America,* Bradley, ed., 2, 118 (1955), quoted by Huntington, supra Note 7 at 4; and Huntington at 5.

82. Huntington, supra Note 7 at 46.

83. Huntington, supra Note 7 at 47.

84. For one possible way of overcoming this barrier, see Witherspoon, *Administrative Implementation of Civil Rights,* esp. 27 ff. (1968).
85. In part, this is so because access to franchise is not equivalent to access to political power. And the frustrations of political impotence will not be dissipated by occasionally depressing the lever in a voting booth. Were the belief in one man-one vote to be truly serious, we would now be exploring not space but the applicability of the available technologies for direct participatory democracy. On such a possibility, see *Harvard University Program on Technology and Society,* Fourth Annual Report 56 ff. (1967–1968).
86. On the possibilities of such control, see Garrity, "Citizen Participation in Government," 3 *Suffolk L. Rev.* 277 (1969).

Direct Action: Definition, Justifications and Explanations

1. Nothing is implied about the wisdom of insurrection or the merits of proposed changes.
2. Processes are democratic if they gratify majority desires, including desires for change of government, without impairing civil rights and minority political rights. I must forego elaborating on the definition of democracy and refer to my discussion in Ross and van den Haag, *The Fabric of Society,* Chaps. 46–47 (1957).
3. A decision against it—however unwelcome to supporters of change—is not evidence of lack of democracy.
4. Such institutions cannot be usefully characterized as democratic or not. For "democratic" when applied to other than political institutions is unilluminating. In a "democratic" family, orchestra, hospital, school, church, firm or university who votes on what? Functionally political organizations, such as labor unions, may have processes analogous to democracy, but not institutions requiring expert guidance, or in which participants have basically different functions, competences, and investments.
5. That sit-ins have been tolerated and that some formerly illegal direct actions, such as strikes, have become legal does not argue for the legalization of any or of all. Concerted abstention from work, unlike the occupation of a building, does not directly and physically impinge on the rights, the privacy and the movement of others. Nevertheless, it is becoming steadily clearer that strikes have to be severely limited in the interest of society; sit-ins certainly must remain illegal, since they are inconsistent with essential property rights.

6. Quoted by Daniel P. Moynihan, *Maximum Feasible Misunderstanding: Community Action in the War on Poverty* (1969)—a brilliant analysis of the community-action programs.

7. Ignoring de Tocqueville's dictum: ". . . the mere fact that certain abuses have been remedied draws attention to the others and they now appear more galling; people may suffer less, but their sensibility is exacerbated . . ."; ignoring, i.e., the obvious fact that the riots were caused by the improvement of the condition of the rioters, the commission followed its guilt-ridden conscience, just as medieval preachers were led to conclude that the sins of the populace were responsible for the black plague. However, the (theological) imputation of guilt has not been confused with the (scientific) determination of causes in modern times before the Kerner Commission. Medieval preachers could not help their ignorance of medicine. The Kerner Commission's ignoring of social dynamics is less excusable. *U.S. National Advisory Commission on Civil Disorders: Report.* (1968).

8. According to the U.S. Census Bureau 18.4 percent of all families were poor in 1959 and 10.7 percent in 1967. Poor white families declined from 15.1 percent of all white families to 8.4 percent; non-whites from 49.5 percent to 30.7 percent of all non-white families. In the same period, the median income of white families rose 46.6 percent, that of non-white families 76.2 percent.

9. Academic intellectuals inclined to play with direct action are concentrated in the softer social sciences and the humanities. (The relationship is mutual: they also soften the sciences they profess.) But many physicists, biologists, linguists, et al. also express their unused guilt feelings (and the vague fear that life has passed them by) by supporting the direct action of their students. They do not test the alleged evils of our society, their avoidability, the remedies, the alternatives, or the effectiveness of the means used to introduce alternatives by the rational, let alone the scientific, criteria they use in their specialties. Moral indignation seems a sufficient method for dealing with the social order. Reason, study and knowledge are not required as they are for, say, embryology or physiology. Indeed, moral indignation may suffice to relieve the specialist's unhappiness—at the expense of those who are the ostensive object of his humanitarian impulse. One should suspect physicians who offer moral enthusiasm instead of medical knowledge. However sincere and moving their pity and concern, not even iatrogenic diseases are cured by it.

10. Black students do not seem to grasp the self-defeating character of the shelter from academic standards they try to build. Afro-American institutes are not likely to yield them useful, let alone marketable skills

or even prestigious degrees—least when they are student controlled and racially staffed. Some militants and the staff might benefit. Other blacks will in time realize that they do not; they will also realize that the universities which endorsed the institutes were derelict in their duty: they did not foster the education of their students but allowed themselves to be pressured by student fanatics and politicians. Children are not grateful, in the end, to meekly permissive parents; they have no reason to be, for the parents did not help them grow up.

11. This definition is based on the results hoped for but confuses them with the process—schooling—which might but need not produce results such as knowledge, refinement, wisdom. Schooling may leave ignorance unimpaired and produce restlessness, unhappiness, boredom, unrealistic ambitions, or worse. The achievement of the intended results appears to be exceptional; it requires gifted pupils, gifted teachers, an appropriate atmosphere—none of which are frequent.

12. In most nonprofessional jobs far more education is required than is used or can possibly be useful. And in many jobs, such as nursing, social work, teaching, the educational requirements are of doubtful relevance to the job. Is it beyond our ingenuity to change this? The misuse of the educational system as an endurance test or as a way to force postponement of entry into the labor market or of guaranteeing guild privileges is contrary to the public interest.

13. In my experience most sociologists and political scientists are amazingly naive—and some quite ignorant—about the basic "philosophical" questions in which many students are more interested than in the often minor technical problems that fascinate their professors. How many are able even to define the economic concept of scarcity or the political concepts of democracy, of freedom or of equality?

14. W. B. Yeats, "To My Daughter."

15. J. M. Keynes, "My Early Beliefs."

16. In America, the Vietnam war may have made a precipitating contribution. But it scarcely explains what happened in France, Germany or Japan.

17. The student selection of heroes expresses the ambivalence produced by the need and craving for discipline and the inability to accept it. There is Paul Goodman (flanked by such a poetic figure as Allen Ginsberg), who spent his life rationalizing his inability to impose any discipline on himself. Full of original and brilliant ideas, as well as of original and silly ideas, Goodman has refused to discriminate between them, i.e., to impose any form of order or discipline on his own mind or production. To him Marx and Freud are aesthetic phenomena. He ignores their ambition to make contributions to the discipline of politi-

cal economy and psychology. Fascinated by the literary and philosophical values of their theories, he uses them indiscriminately as metaphors. He has no interest in exploring the validity of their scientfic contributions by the criteria of the disciplines concerned, and (therefore) has no actual competence to do so. While Goodman appeals through originality, sentimentality, and iconoclastic looseness, the appeal of Herbert Marcuse rests on what appears to be profound and rigorous revolutionary dogmatism. Yet the students confuse rigidity with rigor (Marcuse is innocent of the latter) and pomposity with profundity (Marcuse is not guilty of the latter). They are equally attracted to the appearance (and reality) of non-discipline (Goodman) and to the appearance of discipline (Marcuse).

18. I see no reason why universities need to supervise the noninstructional life of students, provided that students do not insist on university accommodations. Even if they do, they might well be given a decisive voice, provided minority rights and instructional requirements are protected.

19. I have done so to some extent in *The Intercollegiate Review,* Spring 1969.

20. Here too the obvious defects of the university mainly serve as pretexts. The major causes of attack on European universities lie in the spread of egalitarian, antinomian and anti-intellectual, even anti-rational ideology. This ideology is leftist, indeed a bastard offspring of Marxism, Leninism and anarchism. But it defies the communists no less than the other social authorities. Its heroes are the romanticized images of Che Guevara and Mao, one suspects, because of their exotic irrelevance. European student movements share the basic source—the pace and the effects of change in industrialized society—with the American one, but differ in important respects which cannot be examined here. The same must be said for the student movements in communist countries except that the students there are largely concerned with achieving the liberties held in contempt by the activist students in democratic societies who lack the experience of doing without them.

21. See Michael Holroyd, "Harvard on my Mind," 239 *Harper's* 69, (August 1969), or the faculty discussions prompted by the events at Columbia University.

22. It is seldom understood that the last two were reactions to the weakening of authority.

23. This craving is characteristic of American society and was noted alike by de Tocqueville and David Riesman.

24. I am well aware that only about 2 percent of the total student body were activists, according to John T. Roche (*The New Leader,* June 23,

1969). But they were leaders. And administrations and faculties did not have the wit to isolate them—even though the rest of the student body, if supported by the administration, might well have reduced the activists to impotence.

25. This professional attitude is well exemplified in Eric Bentley's dialog with Robert Brustein (*The New Republic,* April 26, 1969, May 17, and ff.) and in the subsequent reaction of professorial letter writers (ibid.).

26. This idea originated in the immunities of European universities. It never existed in the law or practice of the United States. It was intended to protect academic freedom, not to allow its destruction.

27. I am not contending that the university curriculum and didactic procedure could not stand vast improvement. Student ideas may contribute to such improvement. There is no reason not to listen seriously. Yet whatever ideas have so far been advanced would, if at all feasible, make matters worse. (The "free" student-dominated universities have produced nothing but hot air.) To be sure, things could be better and should be made better. But change can also make them worse; and what students so far have advocated, produced, or, through direct action, done, has made matters worse and threatens to make them still worse.

28. The discredit for it belongs to Herbert Marcuse, who derived it from his reading of Marx (I would guess via Lenin).

29. July 5, 1969.

30. I have not dwelled on academic freedom in this essay because I have nothing to add to my views as expressed in "Academic Freedom in the United States," 28 *Law and Contemp. Probs.* 515 (1963).

Direct Action on Campus

1. "What They Believe," 79 *Fortune* 70 ff. (Jan. 1969). The survey of 718 persons between 18 and 24 was conducted for *Fortune* magazine by the Yankelovich organization.

2. Rukeysey, "How Youth is Reforming the Business World," 79 *Fortune* 76 at 142 (Jan. 1969). On the willingness to work in business, even big business, see Riesman, "Where is the College Generation Headed?" in Lloyd-Jones and Estrin, eds., *The American Student and His College,* 6 (1967) reprinted from *The Atlantic Monthly* (1961).

3. See Note 1 at 175.

4. Peterson, "The Student Left in American Higher Education," *Daedalus* 293 (Winter 1968).

5. Glazier, "The Jewish Role in Student Activism," in 79 *Fortune* 112. (Jan. 1969).

6. Kerr, "Towards the More Perfect University," in *The University in America*, 9 at 11 (1967). An Occasional Paper by the Center for the Study of Democratic Institutions.

7. Seligman, "A Special Kind of Rebellion," 79 *Fortune* 66 at 68 (Jan. 1969); see also "The Many Voices of the New Left," a report of the SDS National Convention in 1968. 158 *New Republic* 12 (June 29, 1968).

8. *New York Times*, May 5, 1969, p. 1, col. 3.

9. Hall, "A Conversation with Kenneth Keniston," 2 *Psychology Today*, 16 at 23 (Nov. 1968).

10. See, e.g., the comments on Cuban students in Hochschild, "Student Power in Action," 6 *Trans-Action* 16 (Apr. 1969).

11. Hall, "Interview with Clark Kerr," 1 *Psychology Today*, 25 at 28 (Oct., 1967).

12. Brennan, "A Judge Looks at Student Dissent," 19 *Harvard Law School Bulletin* 9 (Nov. 6, 1968).

13. Leach, *A Runaway World* (1968).

14. On the factions and ideologies of the movement, see Duberman, review of Lasch, *The Agony of the American Left*, in *New York Times Book Review*, Sec. 7, March 23, 1969, p. 1.

15. Keniston, "You have to Grow up in *Scarsdale* to Know How Bad Things Really Are," *New York Times Magazine* 27 (April 27, 1969).

16. *Students and Society*, esp. 45 and 59 (1967). An Occasional Paper by the Center for the Study of Democratic Institutions.

17. See Note 9 at 16.

18. For comparable statements from students and involved faculty see "Comments from Some Combatants," 222 *The Atlantic* 66 ff. (Oct. 1968); in the same issue, see also Parier, "The War Against the Young," at 55. Also, see Duberman, "On Misunderstanding Student Rebels," 222 *Atlantic* 63 (Nov. 1968).

19. See Park, "Alma Mater, Emerita," in *The University in America*, 17 at 19 (1967). An Occasional Paper by the Center for the Study of Democratic Institutions.

20. "Jean-Paul Sartre Talks to Danny the Red," 16 *Atlas* 22 (July 1968); translated from *Die Zeit*, Hamburg.

21. See Note 9 at 19.

22. See Seeman, "The Alienation Hypothesis," 3 *Psychiatry and Social Science Review* 2 (April 1969).

23. Duberman, "Black Power and the American Radical Tradition," in *Dissent: Explorations in the History of American Radicalism*, ed. by Young, 301 at 312 (1968).

24. See Note 5 at 126.

25. See Flacks, "Student Activists: Result, Not Revolt," 1 *Psychology Today* 20 (Oct. 1967).

26. See Note 9 at 19 ff.

27. See Glazier, Note 5 at 126; Birren and Bengtson, "The Young, the Old, the In-Between," 2 *The Center Magazine* 84 (Mar. 1969); also Keniston, *Young Radicals: Notes on Committed Youth* (1968).

28. For further reference to the Sartre interview with Cohn-Bendit see Seale and McConville, *Red Flag/Black Flag   The French Revolution* 17–18, 78 (1968).

29. On the different meanings and types of anarchism, see Note 23 at 310 ff.

30. See Note 4; Peterson distinguishes six types: collegiates, ritualists, academics, intellectuals, left-activists, and hippies. Also, see Kelman, "Beyond New Leftism," 47 *Commentary* 67 (Feb. 1969).

31. Barzun, *The American University* (1968).

32. Ways, "The Faculty is the Heart of the Trouble," 79 *Fortune* 94 at 162 ff. (Jan. 1969).

33. Barzun, "The University as the Beloved Republic," in the *University in America*, 24 at 26 (1967). An Occasional Paper by the Center for the Study of Democratic Institutions.

34. See Note 32 at 162.

35. President Nixon is reported to have written to Father Hesburgh complimenting him on his "forthright stand." *Time* 49 (April 18, 1969). It seems to me that Father Hesburgh was able to do as he did, in part because he knew what was the condition of his institution and he wanted to keep it; his position was strengthened because he wanted to maintain the status quo on at least some matters. Brzezinski suggests that authorities commit typical errors when faced with a revolutionary situation because "they are status quo oriented" and therefore "display an incapacity for immediate effective response." On the contrary, I suggest that the incapacity to act is due to uncertainty about what their status is rather than because the authorities are status quo oriented. See Brzezinski, "Revolution and Counter-revolutions (But not Necessarily about Columbia!)" 158 *The New Republic* 23, esp. 24 (June 1, 1968).

36. For details see Fowler, "A Strange War in Which All Sides Won," 67 *The Pennsylvania Gazette* 6 (Mar. 1969).

37. As Altbach indicates, the earliest campus incidents at Berkeley and Berlin developed out of very minor problems, where the "administrators felt it necessary to demonstrate their 'control' over the institution. . . ." Altbach, "Students Confront the Universities," 32 *The Progressive* 17 (Dec. 1967).

38. See Hechinger, "Student Targets: Professors are Next," 1 *Change* 36 (Jan.–Feb. 1969).

39. For an especially interesting critique of Marcuse, see Bykhovskii, "Marcusism Against Marxism: A Critique of Uncritical Criticism," 30 *Phil. and Phenomonological Research* 203 (1969).

40. See Note 28 at 24 ff.

41. See Friedenberg, *Coming of Age in America*, esp. Chap. II (1963).

42. From the A.A.U.P. model statement on student rights and responsibilities.

43. Wayne State University, *Student Handbook* 138 (1968–1969).

44. Hook also urges such guidelines; see Letter to the Editor, *New York Times*, April 27, 1969, Sec. E., p. 17.

45. The so-called Mundheim report is commented upon in "What to do About Demonstrations?" 66 *Pennsylvania Gazette* 6 (July–August 1968).

46. 394 U.S. 905 (1969). It would require a long, separate essay to deal with the questions of due process for students when they are subject to regulation or discipline by the university. See, e.g., Goldman, "The Universities and the Liberties of its Students—A Fiduciary Theory," 54 *Ky. L. J.* 643 (1966); Van Alstyne, "Students' Academic Freedom and the Rule-Making Powers of Public Universities: Some Constitutional Considerations," 2 *Law in Transition Quart.* 1 (1965); "Symposium: Student Rights and Campus Rules," 54 *Calif. L. Rev.* 1 ff. (1966); 45 *Denver L. J.* 497 ff. (Special 1968), the issue devoted to legal aspects of student-institutional relationships.

47. *Barker v. Hardway*, 283 F.S. 228, 234 (1968).

48. See Saltonstall, "Toward a Strategy of Disruption," in *Students and Society*. An Occasional Paper by the Center for the Study of Democratic Institutions, 28 and 43 (1967).

49. McEvoy and Miller, " 'On Strike—Shut it Down' The Crisis at San Francisco State," 6 *Trans-Action*, 18, 21 (Mar. 1969).

50. See Note 28 at 30–31.

51. On the shift from the civil liberties position in favor of free speech to the fascist position of moral absolutism, see, e.g., Deane, "Reflections on Student Radicalism" in Avory, *Up Against the Ivy Wall*, 285 (1969); also see, "The Moral Right to Impose on Others," Chap. V, in Frankel, *Education and the Barricades*, 60 ff. (1968).

52. Very pertinent is the statement of a group of Fellows, "Student Protests: A Phenomenon for Behavioral Sciences Research," 161, *Science* 20 at 20 and 21 (July 5, 1968).

. . . Antioch's Behavior Research Laboratory (BRL)—was picketed and forcibly closed for a few hours by a group of students because of its research contracts with the Department of Defense. Harry Jerison . . . wrote a statement presenting his position on this entire matter. . . . His concluding paragraphs were a direct response to the student activists who had organized an *ad hoc* Committee Against Defense Research (CADRE). They are worth repeating:

"It may come as a surprise to CADRE, but it is a fact that the Defense Department has always supported many activities of questionable benefit to the military establishment but of great benefit to the country and the world. Beginning with the manning and organizaion of the Lewis and Clark expeditions, continuing through the great geological, paleontological surveys of the 19th century, and into our own time with the support of contracts like the one permitting BRL to exist, the Defense Department and its forbears have been favored instruments for making national commitments to scientific activities. For myself, I would prefer a more honest system. It might make better sense to limit the Defense Department to soldiering, and to develop other approaches to the nonmilitary jobs. However, since the support of unclassified research that I would find acceptable for Antioch is completely aboveboard, with the expenditure and work open for all to inspect, I hesitate to quibble about the words one uses to describe the source of money. It comes out of our tax dollar, and I sometimes think that those who feel guilty about the fraction of their dollar going into military expenditures could be solaced to some extent to learn that the "military" expenditure goes into many nonmilitary activities. The expenditure of taxes that paid for the Naval Academy operations in the 1870's educated Midshipman Michelson. It paid his salary after graduation while he taught at Annapolis and did his first experiments on the speed of light. The Navy Department in this way supported work important enough to merit the first Nobel Prize in Science awarded to an American.

I consider the danger of external control through contracts to be great enough to support regular reviews of contractual commitments. On the whole I have faith that most of the faculty and many of the students have sturdy enough characters to resist selling out. The CADRE group, were it in control, would be much more dangerous. It would first police our morals by making sure that it is impossible for us to sell out to the Defense Department. Next year it could decide that doing research on nucleic acids is irrelevant and therefore immoral, and prohibit that. The scientifically trained members of the community could then be mobilized to work on high priority problems identified by the New Antioch. According to CADRE, Antioch might start by marching its scientists out in a phalanx for action-research on the problems of middle-class ennui in a decadent America. It is an interesting prospect."

Also see Morison, "Foundations and Universities," and Rossi, "Research, Scholars and Policy Makers: The Politics of Large Scale Research," *Daedalus* (Fall 1964).

53. For one interesting interpretation of honesty or objective academic work, see Kriegel, "Playing It Black," 1 *Change* 7 (Mar.–Apr. 1969). See also, Brameld, "The Quality of Intellectual Discipline in America", 378 *The Annals* 75 (1968).

54. For one such experiment, see the various comments on the College at Old Westbury, "The College That Students Helped Plan," 1 *Change* 12 ff. (Mar.–Apr. 1969).

55. Jencks and Riesman, *The Academic Revolution,* esp., Chap. III, "Social Stratification and More Higher Education" (1968). The problem is exacerbated because the need to make deliberate choices between equality and achievement in higher education will increase as knowledge about the educating process accumulates and as access to technological devices for implementing decisions increases. See on this the *Report of the Harvard University Program on Technology and Society* (1967–1968), esp., "Technology's Challenge to Values," p. 53 ff.

56. The Harvard overseers are reported as having "unequivocally supported President Pusey's decision to call the police." *Harvard Today*, 2 (Spring 1969). This special edition of *Harvard Today* contains a detailed account of the Harvard incident.

57. *New York Times*, April 28, 1969, p. 17, col. 3. Also, see "Does an All Black College Make Educational Sense," 2 *Center Magazine* 7 ff. (Mar. 1969).

58. Hand, *The Spirit of Liberty* 34 (1952). The quotation is from a commencement address made in 1927.

59. The inability to see this justification because of the nebulousness helps explain, I think, the conservative reaction, typified in many ways in Kennan, *Democracy and the Student Left* (1968).

Biographical Notes

Tom C. Clark

Associate Justice of the Supreme Court of the United States, nominated to that Court by President Truman in 1949 and retired in 1967. He received his A.B. degree in 1921 and his LL.B. in 1922 at the University of Texas. He has received honorary degrees from 22 universities throughout the country.

He joined the U.S. Department of Justice in 1937 and was named Attorney General by President Truman in June 1945. He is a member of the American, Dallas, Texas, and Federal Bar associations (president 1944–1945); chairman, Board of Directors, National College of State Trial Judges (presented Honorary Life Membership in 1962); fellow, Institute of Judicial Administration, president 1966–1968; member American Judicature Society Board of Directors 1958–1959, chairman, 1967–69; member President's Commission for Observance of Human Rights Year 1968 (chairman Law Committee); chairman Advisory Committee to the National Commission on Reform of Federal Criminal Laws; first director, Federal Judicial Center, Washington, D.C., 1968–69.

Ernst van den Haag

Presently Adjunct Professor of Social Philosophy at New York University and lecturer in sociology and psychology in the graduate and undergraduate faculties at the New School for Social Research. Dr. van den Haag studied at the Universities of Florence, Naples, and the Sorbonne as well as at New York University, where he was granted the Ph.D. degree in 1952. He is a practicing psychoanalyst, a fellow of the American Sociological Association and of the Royal Economic Society and has been a Guggenheim fellow.

He is the author of *Education as an Industry*, 1956, *The Fabric of Society*, 1957 (with Ralph Ross), *Passion and Social Constraint*, 1963, and *The Jewish Mystique*, 1969.

In addition he has contributed chapters to a large number of important books, among them *Mass Culture*, edited by White and Rosenberg; *Psychoanalysis, Scientific Method and Philosophy*, edited by Sydney Hook; *Religious Experience and Truth*, edited by Sydney Hook; *Culture for the Millions*, edited by Norman Jacobs; *The American Scholar Reader*, 1960; *Psychoanalysis in the Social Sciences*, edited by Ruitenbeek; *History and Philosophy*, edited by Sydney Hook; and numerous others.

He has also been a prolific contributor to learned and to belletristic journals, including *Fortune, Harpers, Esquire, Commentary*, and the *Atlantic Monthly*.

Charles V. Hamilton

After a B.A. degree at Roosevelt College and a J.D. degree at Loyola, Dr. Hamilton completed the M.A. and Ph.D. degrees in political science at the University of Chicago. With Stokely Carmichael he published *Black Power*, and he has written

Minority Politics in the Black Belt. In addition he has contributed to numerous professional and popular periodicals.

He has taught at Lincoln University, Rutgers University, Tuskegee Institute, Albany State College, Roosevelt University and is presently professor in the Department of Government at Columbia University. He is also consultant to NBC News on the urban crisis in America.

Samuel I. Shuman

Educated at the University of Pennsylvania (Ph.D.), the University of Michigan (J.D.), and Harvard University (S.J.D.). Since 1951 he has been on the faculty of the Law School of Wayne State University and since 1967 also on the faculty of the Department of Psychiatry in the Medical School. He has also taught and lectured at universities in Europe.

He is the author of *Legal Positivism,* 1963, and in 1966, with N.D. West, the translator of *The Austrian Penal Act,* in *The American Series of Foreign Penal Codes.* He edited *The Future of Federalism,* 1968, and, also 1968, with Gray Dorsey, edited and contributed to *Validation of New Forms of Social Organization.* In addition he has contributed to other books and to numerous journals both in America and abroad. He is the American editor of *Archives for Philosophy of Law and Social Philosophy* and is on the Editorial Board of the *American Journal of Jurisprudence.*

Index

Academic freedom, and student activism, 115

Assassination, expected and unexpected, 133

Audience reaction, and freedom of speech, 54-58, 74, 82

Black studies programs, demand for, 185

Civil disobedience, necessity for, 40; and orderliness, 51-52; possible legitimacy of, 39-41; right of, 41; by state governors, 23, 41-42

Civil rights, biracial efforts, 134; pursuing only legal remedies, 136-137

College education, availability of, 105; deteriorating quality of, 105-106; extent of, 143-144; relevance of, 105, 116

Conduct, exclusion under First Amendment, 61; as resistance, 39; as speech, 13, 50, 58, 60-67, 75-76

Direct action, antidemocratic, 98-99; appropriateness of objective, 167-168; defined, 97; early history of in U.S., 20-21; first great victory of, 22; judicial approval of, 19; in labor disputes, 22; legitimation of, 34, 97-99, 130, 166-172; by orderly marching, 51, 66; relation of objective to method, 168; as resistance, 39; by state officials, 23, 41-42, 92; strategies of, 85, 130, 172; as supplement to legal actions, 128

Expressive conduct, and anonymity, 84-85; appropriate place for, 67-70, 73; burning draft card, 62-64, 66; and disruption, 85-86; by use of the flag, 61-62; and obscenity, 79, 83; picketing, 66; and protected speech, 59-61, 75-84; psychology of, 14; trespassing, 81-82; and violence, 14, 86-88

Faculty, apathy about administration, 161, 164-165; declining commitment to the university, 158-161

Fourteenth Amendment, and the Bill of Rights, 44-45; early limitations by the Supreme Court, 21

Fascism, American rejection of, 93; of the left or right, 93, 187; in the universities, 178-179, 187

233

The manuscript was edited by Alexander Brede. The book jacket was designed by Mary Jowski. The type face for the text is Linotype Baskerville designed by John Baskerville in the Eighteenth Century, and the display face is Bulmer.

The text is printed on S. D. Warren's Olde Style Antique paper and the book is bound in Elephant Hide paper over binder's board. Manufactured in the United States of America.